FEELING
THE
FUTURE

Use the power of your brain & heart to
find your way in the unknown and
achieve your life & business goals with ease

TYLER P. MONGAN
www.tylermongan.com

www.mindlabmethod.com

FEELING THE FUTURE: Use the power of your brain & heart to find your way in the unknown and achieve your life & business goals with ease

Copyright © *Tyler P Mongan,* tylermongan.com. *All Rights Reserved. First Edition, 2018.*

Cover and Interior Design by Tyler P Mongan

ISBN-13: 978-0-692-16347-4

In this book you will learn methods, concepts, & mind states for Feeling The Future to produce tangible outcomes. You will explore experiments that leverage the power of your brain, heart, & body to help you achieve your goals with ease and get more from your life and business, fast. With these new techniques and perspectives, you will join a growing community of people who are creating a frictionless future where anything is possible.

FEELING
THE
FUTURE

CONTENTS

INTRODUCTION | **5**

Chapter 1: FEELING THE FUTURE | **19**

Chapter 2: FEELINGS | **45**

Chapter 3: GOALS | **65**

Chapter 4: THE FIVE STEP METHOD | **95**

    Full Version of Mind Lab Method | **97**

    Simplified Version of Mind Lab Method | **130**

Chapter 5: EXPERIMENTS | **141**

Chapter 6: 10 LESSONS LEARNED | **159**

CONCLUSION | **191**

PREFACE

Feeling The Future is a record of the extraordinary experiences and important lessons learned from hosting the **Mind Lab Method: the Science of Goal Setting** around the world. Since its 2015 launch in Hawaii, I have personally shared these methods with hundreds of entrepreneurs, business owners, and thought leaders around the world, who came together at **Mind Lab Method** workshops to gain clarity about their goals, discover new goals, develop timelines for success, and feel more confidence about the future. The **Mind Lab Method** is based on neuroscience and patterned on the scientific method. It is integrated with leading edge heart-brain communication research, cognitive social behavior, and mindfulness practices. The goal of the **Mind Lab Method** is to disseminate these tools and techniques for architecting the future.

The results from the **Mind Lab Method** are consistent and reliable across languages, cultures and areas of emphasis. In the process of fine tuning the tools, techniques and methods for thinking about the future, my own work matured and expanded into training corporate executives around the globe on coherent leadership, actionable innovations, and future intelligence.

Feeling the Future will provide you with tools, mindsets, and experiments to explore your own goals and future. In this book, I will share the **Mind Lab Method** in a step-by-step framework, along with 10 of the most important and practical lessons that I have learned from hosting the event around the world. All the content is based on real life experience, not theory.

You can apply the ideas and practices in your own life immediately. I encourage you to experiment: without the fear of failure or the desire for success. Be willing to explore the uncertain and the unknown. You can record your goals, notes, and results in this book. You can return to the process over and over as you learn to Feel the Future and create your life and business.

The future is X, an unknown. The future is an experiment. If you are not experimenting and creating your own future, then you are living someone else's future.

As you read, keep these two important things in mind:
1. We are all just making it up. If you are not making up your own future, then someone is making it up for you.
2. The more people who benefit from the future you make up, the faster it will become a reality.

The Future is X. Anything is Possible.

INTRODUCTION

Consider this...if you felt happy, powerful, & free, what types of goals would you have?

Let's do an experiment to find out. Take a moment, right now, and feel the feelings of being happy, powerful, & free in your body. You can start by simply thinking the words and thoughts of "happy, powerful, & free." Notice what feels different. Notice how your body starts to change as you feel the feelings of happy, powerful, & free.

In this state, ask yourself, "what are my goals *right now*?"

Notice what emerges.

When you feel happy, powerful, & free, you don't really need much else. And when you don't need much, then goals become less important, or the types of goals you have are very different than the goals you had in the past. Do you think it would be easier to accomplish your goals when you feel happy, powerful, & free? And wouldn't any goal that aligns with those feelings be enjoyable to accomplish?

Goals are a journey, not a destination. When you find the *feeling* behind your goals and activate that feeling in your body, then in a real, physical way the goal has already been achieved. When you maintain that *feeling* in the body and that physical state associated with the goal, then it becomes easier to make that goal a reality…moving it from the mind into physical matter.

Feelings prepare your brain and physiology for some future event to happen, so that your body is ready to take action when the moment arises. By embodying the future in the present moment you increase the probability that a specific possibility will become a reality. When you learn how to *feel the future*, your body aligns with the things you want in your life and business, and there is less resistance to them appearing in your life.

I know this because I constantly test and experiment with the concepts in this book while teaching others how to apply them in their life and business. While working around the world with entrepreneurs, corporate teams, and individuals like you, I consistently see positive, surprising results.

Here's an example. While attending the Mind Valley A-fest event in Mykonos, Greece, I set a goal to practice the feeling of being a speaker in front of a large audience, even though I was not speaking at the event. I continually maintained that state of being as I met new people and enjoyed the workshops and parties.

As I was engaging people, I recall one person asked me, "when are you presenting at A-fest?" because they said they really wanted to attend my talk. Another person approached me and apologized for missing my presentation, as they had really wanted to attend. And even after the event I received a facebook message, from a third person, asking if there was a recording of my presentation to watch. But I was not a speaker at the event! Rather I was holding the feelings and the state of being of a speaker at the event. Interestingly, these feelings were having a real world effect on others.

When you learn how to access the feelings behind your goals, then you can understand what you really want from life. This understanding is not just psychological or metaphysical; rather, it is a full-body, physiological understanding. After all, your entire body must go with you into the future (at least for now). As you embody new states of being you can also discover new goals and ideas about your future that you have never thought about before. And that is when all the real magic starts to happen.

Goals are important, but not in the way we typically think about them. Goals are enlightening us to feelings we want to embody so that new possibilities in the future can be realized. As we strive toward a goal, we transform into a new person. We become the person that can achieve the goal. In the process of changing into a new person, our goals may change and that is okay, because the original goal is not really what we wanted in the first place.

Goals are not the end. They are the start of a journey deeper into the self. Goals are a realization of feelings that we have been missing in our life. It is this journey that allows the future, and the future you, to emerge in expected and unexpected ways.

I trust you will enjoy this book. Aloha to your future. May it be preferred and purposeful. Be Happy. Feel Powerful. Live Free.

Tyler P. Mongan

> **EXPERIMENT: Get 33% closer to achieving your goal right now!**
>
> 1. Think of a goal you have over the next two weeks.
> 2. Now think of the feelings you will have when you accomplish the goal.
> 3. Find those feelings in the body right now.
> 4. Continue to feel those feelings of the goal being accomplished and maintain that feeling, over and over again.

THIS IS AN EXPERIMENT…WORLD TOUR

In 2013-2014, I was the Director of Operations for Smart Sustainability Consulting (SSC) in Hawaii. We developed a unique energy intelligence and education behavior change program for clients including the Department of Education and the Department of Defense. During the programs, we shared lighting, temperature, and plug-load information to change participants' perceptions around energy use and then mentored them during a month-long audit of their buildings. The program participants realized that information, experiential learning, collaboration, and small changes can have huge impact on energy reduction goals.

After running the program for about a year at schools and military bases, SSC had helped the state of Hawaii identify over $8,000,000 — eight million dollars — through changing energy use behavior. The program was a huge success, and I wondered if some of the same techniques could be used to help entrepreneurs get better at changing their behaviors to achieve their business goals.

After my time at SSC I consulted on a few projects until the end of 2014. I began to feel that there was something new emerging in my future and I needed to get ready for that future to become a reality. I did not know exactly what this future looked like, but I asked myself a simple question, "What do I need to do to get ready for the future?"

Ideas started to come. For example, "sell my car, get rid of stuff, and keep my living situation flexible." As I took action on these ideas the future started to become clear. I could see that I was going to be traveling and teaching something that was similar to the work I did at SSC, but also very different.

I began to collaborate on these ideas with Jonathan Fritzler,[1] who was on the business development team for

---

[1] You can find out more about Jonathan Fritzler's work at: www.jonathanfritzler.org and www.mindlab.institute

SSC. We both had a passion for helping people start businesses and expand their minds. Our intention was to develop a process to help entrepreneurs gain clarity about their life and business goals and develop strategies to achieve them fast.

I revisited my background in medicine and science and began reading the latest in scientific research concerning goal-setting. This research lead to deeper exploration into neuroscience, heart-brain communication, and quantum theory. I integrated my personal experience in professional development and Lean Startup methods with what I discovered in the scientific literature. The end result was **Mind Lab: The Science of Goal Setting.** In alignment with its scientific grounding, we called the initial events: Mind Lab "This is an experiment."

About three-months before the official launch of the Mind Lab experiment, I awoke one morning with the idea that we needed to do a West Coast U.S. Tour to launch the Mind Lab concept into the world. Applying Lean Startup philosophy we soon hosted the first Mind Lab Experiment in Hawaii, and that same evening caught a flight for the U.S. West Coast.

We applied the Mind Lab process to develop our tour goals and strategy: 10 cities, 10 Mind Lab experiments, and $10,000. In three months.

Within the first week of the tour we had already achieved our $10,000 goal by landing a consulting client. By the end of the tour we had hosted 16 Mind Lab "experiments" in 10 cities and engaged hundreds of people. We had exceeded all our goals.

During the tour, we were able to rapidly prototype and test different concepts of the Mind Lab experiment to discover which ones were the most valuable. The process was fine-tuned into a solid framework that now serves as the basis for the **Mind Lab Method**.

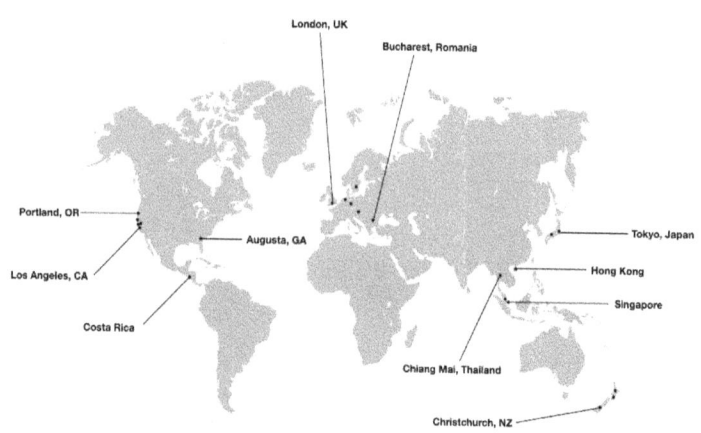

(Image 0) Sample of Mind Lab Tour Locations.

The West Coast U.S. tour was only the beginning. Due to the incredible positive feedback, I just kept traveling and facilitating. Since launching the Mind Lab Experiment in the US I have personally hosted it in cities across the globe with similar results regardless of language or culture.

Mind Lab participants report greater clarity about their goals, more confidence about their future and more focused energy to achieve things fast. The **Mind Lab Method** takes participants on a journey into the mind and heart, and helps them to cultivate a physiological relationship with the future of their life and business.

Maybe you have never had a goal, or maybe you have Really Big Goals. I have personally seen the Mind Lab help with both cases, and everything in between. The method will help you access what really matters to you right now and allow you to use that feeling to create your future.

The **Mind Lab Method** challenges you to think differently. It is like yoga for the mind. Just like yoga, you do not go to one yoga class and give up; you keep practicing and you improve slowly over time. The method is designed to stretch the mind and help you realize new possibilities, access untapped potentials. The method prepares your brain & body for the actions to make your goals a reality.

You are probably reading this because you have a goal in mind that you want to achieve. To achieve that goal you have to change and become someone different, and that can be scary and feel dangerous to the brain. The brain is designed to prevent change because change leads to uncertainty and the unknown. To further complicate things, when you change, the familiar and old you no longer exists and that can make people, especially those closest to you, feel uncomfortable.

In the process of achieving your goal you may become someone completely different than the person you are right now. You may speak, stand, and walk differently. You may have new clothes and new friends. When you change internally, your external world changes too.

The good thing is, you don't have to do this. You are free to give up and go back to being your old self at any time! If you don't want to think differently and change, then this book is probably not for you. You have the power to choose. If you choose to explore new future possibilities and become a different person who is happy, feels powerful, & lives free, then join me, join all of us, in feeling the future.

Books that have inspired this work[2]

1. "You are the Placebo" by Joe Dispense
2. "The Intention Experiment" by Lynn Mcttagart
3. "Biology of Belief" by Bruce Lipton
4. "The Values Factor: The Secret to Creating an Inspired and Fulfilling Life" by De Martini
5. "The Living Universe" by Duane Elgin
6. "Heart Intelligence" by Doc Childre, Howard Martin, Deborah Rozman, and Rollin McCraty
7. "The Hearts Code" - by Paul Pearsall
8. "The New Science of Life' by Rupert Sheldrake
9. "Limitless Mind" by Russel Targ
10. "Pscyho-cybernetics" by Maxwell Maltz
11. "As a Man Thinketh" by James Allen
12. "The One Thing" by Gary W. Keller and Jay Papasan
13. "Mind: A Journey Into the Heart of Being Human" by Daniel J Siegel

---

[2] See Citations page at end of book for full citation

NOTES

NOTES

It is not about the goal, it is about the person you become in achieving the goal

CHAPTER 1 | **FEELING THE FUTURE**

In 2015, while researching content for the **Mind Lab Method**, I came across the work of Duane Elgin, an American author, speaker, and educator. He had written several books on the future of humanity and started a website documenting "great transition stories," which share ideas about how humanity is transitioning onto a new future trajectory.

Immediately upon discovering Duane's work, I sent him an email. He emailed me back within a few minutes and within one hour, I was on a Skype meeting with Duane (and Mind Lab experiment co-creator Jonathan Fritzler). We had such a great connection that Duane invited us to meet him at his house in California later that month.

During the meeting, we discussed Duane's work and what he saw as the future for humanity. He explained the idea of a great transition in humanity which includes three key features: (1) Humanity is growing up, (2) Humanity is waking up, (3) Humanity is on a new trajectory.[3]

> **Humanity is growing up:** While lecturing around the world, Duane asks the audience, "Is humanity a child, adolescent, or an adult." By far the most common answer is "adolescent." So most people agree that humanity still has room to grow.
>
> **Humanity is waking up:** The internet, technology, and artificial intelligences are rapidly increasing our ability to connect to new information and ideas globally. It is also increasing our ability to connect to each other. The internet is like a collective brain that we can access to learn new things and see what is happening around the world instantly.
>
> **Humanity is on a new trajectory:** Because humanity is growing up and waking up, people are able to envision new ways of living, new ways of governing, and new ways of doing business. Ultimately, people are taking back their personal and collective power to create a new vision of the future. Exactly what it looks like on the other side

---

[3] See www.duaneelgin.com for more of Duane's insights and ideas.

of the transition is still emerging, but we can all be part of architecting this new future.[4]

The idea of the great transition helps frame the current state of humanity. Things are in constant transition. The rapid speed of change is becoming the new norm. When I was a kid, cellular phones, touch screens, video conferencing, drones, robots, and artificial intelligence were science fiction. Now these things are norms, and new, unpredictable norms are arising just as quickly.

This appears to make the future more Volatile, Ambiguous, Complex, and Uncertain (VACU).[5] This VACU future can feel very uncomfortable to the brain as it is constantly trying to predict the future to keep life consistent and ensure survival.

This also makes the future full of new opportunities and possibilities. Technology is helping us to not only develop new products, services, and ways of communicating, but also allowing us to gain a deeper understanding of how the human body works and how we can use science to reach more optimized performance levels in life and business.

---

[4] Duane Elgin, *PROMISE AHEAD: A Vision of Hope and Action for Humanity's Future*, New York: HarperCollins, 2000

[5] VACU was introduced by the U.S. Army War College to describe the future after the end of the Cold War in 1990's. Since then it has been used in business to help frame the context of foresight and horizon scanning.

I often start the **Mind Lab Method** by asking participants, "how many of you have fear, worry, or frustration about the future?" Typically 90% of the participants raise their hands in response. However, by the end of the workshop I ask the same question, and only 20% of the participants raise their hands.

As you take the time to develop more future intelligence, you will learn techniques and start to feel more comfortable with your ability to architect the future. Remember: if you are not creating your future, then someone is creating it for you.

WHAT IS THE FUTURE ANYWAY?

Take a moment and think about the future. What does it mean to you?

Here are some things that may come to mind:

- There are some things in the future that we want to happen, and other things we do not want to happen.
- There are things we think we know are going to happen, and things we think cannot happen.
- There is a sense of change, growth and development.
- The future is emerging and unfolding, and not always clear.
- The future is unknown and uncertain.

- You can't stop the future from coming. There is no pause button.

A simple definition of the future from the dictionary reads, "pertaining to a time after the present," but that doesn't give us much to work with. A quick visit into the world of Future Studies, or futurology, reveals three types of futures:
- Possible futures: what can or could be (usually based on scientific knowledge)
- Probable Futures: what is likely to be (usually based on probabilities and experience)
- Preferable Futures: what ought to be and what seems most appealing (based on personal or group preference)

As you make your way through this book, keep in mind that what we think is possible, probable, and preferable are often determined by our past experience, current neural pathways, and by the lens through which we view the universe. This can support us in achieving a goal and it can also limit us.

For the purposes of this book let's consider two ways to think about the future:
1. The future as purposeful (not just possible, probable, or preferred)
2. The future is part of a scale of certainty and uncertainty, which is really a feeling.

PURPOSEFUL FUTURES

We are all just making it up. When you wake up in the morning, there is nothing you have to do or are supposed to do. Rather, you start thinking, feeling and taking action, often times without much conscious effort. Pause for a moment and consider the reality that you are just making up the future. The next steps you take don't have any real logic behind them, other than the logic of the past. Right now, you can choose to make up any future you want.

Beyond the possible (what could happen), probable (what is likely to happen), and preferred (what you want to happen) futures, there are also purposeful futures. These are futures that we take the time and energy to intentionally create. Not only are they possible, probable, and preferred, they also align with our physiology (brain, heart and body) in a way that makes them an expression of our mental, emotional, and physical understanding of the world.

My work is to help individuals and organizations architect purposeful futures. I teach them how to think about, and feel into, a particular future. This aligns their brain and heart to take action towards a single future. Some people are all thought and no action, so nothing seems to happen for them. And some people are all action and no thought, and although they are always creating new things, they often create futures they do not really want or are not purposeful.

When you are purposeful in creating the future you have a sense of personal power, and a better understanding of where you want to go. You can easily align with where others want to go and you help drive the collective future forward in a more conscious way.

As you dive deeper into this book you will learn techniques to consciously make up your future and architect purposeful collective futures.

FEELING THE FUTURE: CERTAINTY AND UNCERTAINTY

The first thing you need to know about certainty is that it is a mental state as well as a feeling. Certainty is related to your feeling about the quality of a truth and your lack of skepticism about an idea. If you are certain that something happened in the past, then it means you have *no doubt* that it happened. You have a feeling about some event or experience that is often supported by facts, but it does not need to be supported by facts. To the body, feelings matter more than facts.

Most people would agree that the future is uncertain. However, when we speak about the past we typically have experiences we are certain about and others that we are uncertain about. For example, you may be certain about the person you shared your first kiss with, that you went to a specific school, or the city where you were born. On the other hand you are probably not certain about what grade you got on one of your 4th grade math tests or what you had for lunch 482 days ago. Even though we are certain that things happened in the past, we are not always certain of what exactly happened or how they happened.

The important point is that things we are certain about are alive in our physiology and influencing us right now. Things we are less certain about have less influence on us right now. And things we are uncertain about have little or no influence on us right now. For example, if I am certain that I have a bachelor's degree in Biology, then that is a part of me. I can refer to it and it activates a feeling inside me that I completed the degree and that it matters. I can confidently list it on my resume and it might help me get a job.

However, if I am uncertain about something; for example, which seat I sat in during my biochemistry class in college or what score I got on my 3rd genetics quiz, then it has less significance in my life and it matters less.

Interestingly, if I was uncertain that I had a bachelor's degree in Biology, then I would not feel confident listing that on my resume because it is not alive in my physiology, and it does not matter. I cannot rely on it to help me in the moment.

The things that we are certain about play a big role in our understanding of self and our identity. We tend to be more certain about things from the past and we tend to think the future is always uncertain. This means that the past matters more than the future and it has more influence on what is possible.

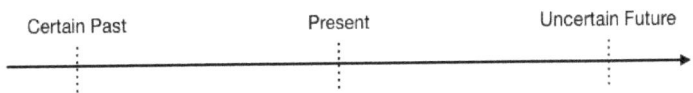

(Image 1.1) Old model of how we feel about the past, present and future. The Past feels certain and fixed. We can feel certain of things in the Present. The Future feels uncertain.

However, there are some things in the future, at least in our immediate future, that we are certain about. For example, if there is a cup of water in front of you in the moment, you are probably certain you can drink it. If you take a sip of the water, you would be certain you drank from the cup. And all this matters to you when you are thirsty.

Take a look a the timeline in image 1.1. You can see that we are usually very certain about things in the present moment. For example, you are certain you are reading these words in this book right now. You are certain what city and location you are in right now. And you are probably certain what date and time it is right now (even if you need to look it up).

Typically we think that in the present moment there is a high level of certainty and in the past there is certainty and uncertainty, with no opportunity to change what has happened. In the future there is uncertainty, and lots of opportunity for change, because nothing has happened yet.

But do you know what city and location you will be in 3 years from now in the same month, day, and time? You are probably not certain about that. When you think about it, you quickly realize you have no clue about where you will be in the future.

At the same time, you could make a choice, right now, to be at a specific location in a specific month, day and time, three years from now. You can create a feeling of certainty that you are going to be there no matter what.

Regardless of the facts, you now have a feeling about the future concerning something that you want to happen. When you say you are certain, then you are stating it will happen, because you are going to make it happen. You could have such a strong feeling of certainty that you will actually make the effort to be in that city in the future, that you would not let anyone or anything block you from making that future a reality…even though it is three years from now.

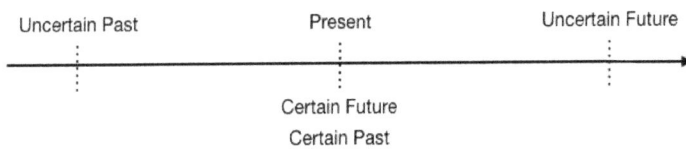

(Image 1.2) New model of how we feel about the past, present and future.

Image 1.2 illustrates that things you are certain about are alive in your physiology in the present moment, even if they are events in the past or in the future. They are anchored in your physiology with the feelings you have about those things and they are influencing your ability to take action.

At the same time, the things you are uncertain about, in the past or future, are not alive in your Now and hence they are not aligned with your physiology. The past does not need to matter more, or be more alive in our physiology, than the future. You can simply shift more of your certainty to future events, instead of applying the feeling of certainty to the past.

In a real way, "you can shift your body from a record of the past, and into a map for the future."[6] The more certain you are of the past, the less energy you have to create a new future. The more certain you are of a future, the more energy you will have to make it a reality.

SUMMARY (OF THE FUTURE)

We can architect purposeful futures. These are well thought-out and well felt-out futures that align with our physiology. When we align our brain, heart, & body to take action towards a particular future, then things can happen faster than we can imagine.

The past, present, and future are simply a feeling of either certainty or uncertainty. As experiences drift further from the present and into the past we become less certain about them. Some experiences in the past we are very certain about and this means the feelings of these experiences still matter to us. Other experiences we feel

---

[6] See www.joedispenza.com for more details.

less certain or uncertain about and those are experiences that don't matter to us.

If we apply this same thinking to the future, then if the future is uncertain, it does not matter to us. The more you can link the feeling of certainty to specific future outcomes the more your body starts to anticipate that future happening. It starts to fire and wire the neural pathways, to stimulate genes, and to produce proteins and hormones as if it is already living in that future, Now. All of this increases the probability that your brain, heart and body will put in the time and energy to make the future idea a reality…to make it matter.

Later in the book you will learn techniques and experiments to feel more certain about future possibilities, while freeing yourself from the limiting certainties of the past. Let me share a personal story with you about freeing myself from the past to create a new future.

DROPPING OUT OF MEDICAL SCHOOL TO FEEL A NEW FUTURE

In 2007, after spending nine years of my life striving towards the goal of becoming a doctor, I dropped out of my third year in medical school. Growing up, I was certain

I would become a doctor, just like my father. I wanted to wear the white coat, have the power to save lives, and, of course, make lots of money. However, during medical school I realized that I had been following the wrong goal and creating the wrong future.

In my second year of medical training I was starting to burn out, and needed a change. So, instead of taking my medical science boards, I decided to take a two week vacation in Hawai'i to study Hawaiian healing methods and relax in the sun on the beach.

Upon landing in Hawai'i I immediately felt a feeling that I had been missing for the past nine years. It was the feeling of home. Later on I would learn from one of my Hawaiian teachers that if you don't know where "home" is then you will always feel lost. By the second week in Hawai'i I was feeling more at home and recharged, with a new motivation to finish medical school.

On my last day in Hawai'i I recall standing between the mountains and ocean (*mauka* and *makai* in Hawaiian) and saying these fateful words, "I feel like I could live here." After that simple statement I knew that something inside me had shifted. I felt different. Even though I had never thought about living in Hawai'i until that moment, I immediately felt like it was a real possibility.

Before boarding the plane back to Arizona, I ran into the husband of a fellow student who happened to have the same flight itinerary as me. He was originally from Hawai'i and asked if I had taken the time to surf during my visit. Unfortunately, I had not had a chance to surf, and at that time I was a little embarrassed to admit I was somewhat afraid of the ocean.

As we boarded the plane together, we heard an announcement over the speakers, "we need two people to give up their seats in exchange for flight vouchers, food, and hotel rooms." We looked at each other and raised our hands to volunteer. He turned to me and said, "I will take you surfing." The next day I surfed my first waves.

I was in love, not only with Hawai'i, but with the feelings it brought me. There was a sense of freedom and also a clear realization that I had been chasing the wrong goal.

Did I really want to be a doctor? Why?

I thought the question through all the way to where it ended with me finally retiring after 30 years of medical practice. Seeing that future self that was finally free to do whatever I wanted to do when I wanted to do it, made we question why I could not have those feelings in my life right now. My brain had been trained to think, "after I work hard and retire, then I am allowed to follow my heart and do what I want. That is how life works."

I asked myself, "what if I retire right now? If becoming a doctor is just a means to the end goal of retiring, then why wait so long to reach the goal?"

My future became more uncertain.

When I returned to Arizona my logical brain took over again and told me to suck it up, be responsible, and finish medical school. I thought to myself, "I have two years left and I have already made it so far." I listened to my logical brain, as I had always done, but soon the feelings of my heart found ways to change my mind.

I recall seeing signs and hearing radio ads for Hawai'i. While driving, a man cut me off in a motorcycle with a "Hard Rock Café Honolulu, Hawai'i" t-shirt on. And the final message came to me when I was looking at a patient's chart and there was a sticky note that said, "this guy is on Hawai'i time."

I knew what I had to do. Regardless of what I thought, or what others thought, I was certain that I had to drop out of medical school and move to Hawai'i. I wanted to learn how to surf, spend time on the beach, and see what would happen if I retired right now (even without money to sustain me long-term). It was one of the most difficult choices of my life, but once I made it, I felt free of the certainty of the past.

I realized several things after dropping out of medical school. First, my goal to become a doctor was not really my goal. Maybe it was me living my father's dream, the American dream, or the rational ideals of my brain. Second, I realized you do not have to become a doctor to help people heal. And third, there was power in feeling. I discovered that the future was not only something you could think about, but it was something you could feel.

Although the flight to my new home in Hawai'i was full of uncertainty and even fear, I felt happy, powerful, & free. I knew I was cultivating a new state of being, becoming a new person and plotting a trajectory into a new future.

In Hawai'i I learned how to surf, studied martial arts, became a yoga instructor, and trained in Oriental Medicine and Acupuncture. I was learning how to find the rhythm in myself and how that aligned with the rhythm of life. I was learning how to feel the future and explore the feelings that had been missing in my life.

As I became a new person I rediscovered my interest in entrepreneurship. I launched organizations in Hawai'i that focused on sustainability and community building. I started a sustainable living resource guide coupon book for local green business called the HonuGuide and co-founded a media company that initially focused on sustainable and action lifestyle (now travel-tourism media) called Nella Media Group.[7]

As I continued to develop my ability to feel the future, more and more amazing things happened. I became the editor of the second most-read publication in Hawai'i overnight and launched the first issue in 30 days, without any previous experience as an editor. I spent five years as a musician playing in a band that was nominated for the Hawaiian music award, Na Hoku Hanohano. I made three albums and played the best venues in Hawai'i, without any musical training. I started a career as a global business leadership trainer and spoke at conferences around the world on Coherent Leadership, Mindful Innovation, and Future Intelligence.

I share these accomplishments because I want you to realize that when you learn how to feel the future with certainty and take purposeful action toward that future, the path from idea to reality shortens, things happen faster than you can imagine, miracles become the norm, and your life is no longer limited by the past.

---

[7] See www.nellamediagroup.com

THE ONE MILLION DOLLAR BRIEF CASE

Our brain and our body are constantly predicting and preparing for the future. This is important for survival because we need to be ready to take action at the first sign of danger.

Although our brain and body are preparing for the future, they are often stuck in the past. If you take a moment and think about something that happened last week that you were excited or happy about, what happens? As you think about that past, your body starts to fire the same neural pathways and release the same hormones associated with the experience. Your thinking brain and feeling body are now in that past experience and they do not know the difference between the past and the present because in a real physical way the past becomes the present.

What would happen if you used the same thinking and feeling to bring your brain and body into the future so that the future becomes the present? Do you think you would be more ready for the future you are thinking about to become a reality?

Sometimes we are not ready for the future that we think we want. At times the brain has a goal or desire, but the rest of your body does not want to cooperate. Other times the body is already feeling a particular future, but our brain resists the possibility of that future becoming a reality.

One experiment I like to run is called Future Tripping *(you can learn the steps in the Experiments section, Chapter 5)*. During the experiment, participants choose a future possibility, or a future miracle that they desire to become a reality. Then they take a trip to find the feeling in the future where the miracle has happened.

The basic idea is that we can prepare the brain and body for a particular future and then practice thinking and feeling the future, activating the thalamus in the brain to integrate our imagination with the senses of the body. This increases the probability that the desired future will become a reality because the feelings of that future possibility become present in the body. The brain's reticular activation system (RAS), the part of the brain that searches for experiences relevant to our survival, is now primed to find ways to make that desired future a reality.

Most people want more money; however when more money appears they may resist taking it. For example, imagine you are leaving work or the gym in the evening and a man approaches you dressed in all black with black gloves and a black brief case. As he approaches you he begins to hand you the black brief case and he says, "here is your one million dollars, take it." He even opens it up enough so you can see the money inside.

The one million dollar question is, would you take the brief case?

Seriously. Would you take the brief case?

Typically people say they would take the briefcase, but if you are honest with yourself then you would consider the following: First, you would probably start to walk away from a man dressed in all black with black gloves and a black briefcase walking right at you in the evening. Second, it is not typical that strangers walk up to us and hand us things, and even less typical that they would hand you a brief case full of money. Third, our brain is trained to look for dangers and risks and avoid them. To the brain, this situation seems very risky. This man must be a criminal or there is a catch to this exchange that you are unaware of.

The reality is, most people would not take the brief case.

However, imagine that just before leaving work or the gym, you took a trip into the future with the thoughts of your mind and the feelings of your body. In that future you noticed a man dressed in all black, with black gloves, walking up to you and handing you a black brief case with one million dollars. Then imagine that you made the image more real as you felt the sensations of what it was like to receive that briefcase and how comfortable and excited you would be during the experience. And then you kept that feeling in your body as if the experience has already happened.

After doing that experiment with your mind and body, you leave your work or the gym in the evening and you walk down the street and a man dressed in all black, with black gloves on, really walks up to you, in real life, and hands you a black briefcase full of one million dollars, *now* would you take the brief case?

Of course you take the briefcase! You practiced the exact future, and you are mentally and physiologically ready for that future to be a reality. The RAS of the brain is looking for that future. There is even a part of you that would expect that future to happen and your brain would not be triggered to question the experience or become alarmed. There would be no physiological resistance to that future. You would take the briefcase with confidence as if it was supposed to happen.

Now, I want to be clear. I am not saying that you actually make that future happen, as if by magic, with your thoughts, feelings and intention. Rather, you increased the possibility that the particular future would be realized by preparing for it. You also reduced your mental and physical resistance to that future happening. When the external conditions arise to allow that future to happen, you are ready for it and you embrace it, just like playing your role in a play.

Often times we miss what is already available to us because our brain is not trained to see it. Or we reject things that we want because we are not ready to receive them. By taking the time to mentally practice the future with the mind, and physically feel the future with the body, then we increase the probability that we will see the future we want when it arises. We will be ready for that future to become a reality. And when we see it we will take action to make it real.

NOTES

NOTES

Language of the mind is thought
Language of the body is feeling

CHAPTER 2 | **FEELINGS**

We have been talking about *Feeling the Future*, the title of this book, but we have not yet considered the concept of feelings. So, what is a feeling?

To maintain homeostasis, our physiology is constantly adjusting in response to internal and external stimuli. A stimulus may trigger an emotional pathway in the body, engaging various neural pathways and releasing a cocktail of hormones and neurochemicals. We can interpret the activation of these emotional pathways as feelings.

For example, if you come across a snake while hiking in the woods, your body will trigger an emotional system in the brain in response to the external stimulus. The heart rate and breath rate will increase, the pupils dilate, and blood moves away from the digestive system and into the skeletal muscles to increase the capacity for movement. The stimulation of this emotional system results in a feeling in the body that may be interpreted as fear or anxiety.

The important thing to keep in mind is that emotions and their associated feelings are not just psychological (mental); rather they are deeply physiological (full body) experiences. The feeling of fear activates physical changes in the body that lead to specific thoughts, feelings, actions and beliefs.

The emotions and feelings that we practice over and over trigger the same hormones and neuropathways to stimulate the genes that make the proteins that are the building blocks for your physical body. This means that the the more we practice a specific feeling the more it becomes the physical foundation of who you are. In a real way these feelings influence your ability to think about the future, to feel the future, and to become someone new in the future.

The key point to keep in mind is that the feelings of your past self are the biggest barrier to feeling a new future self. Let's dive a little deeper into our physiological past and discover why the person you are right now is the biggest barrier to achieving your future goals.

NERVOUS SYSTEM DEVELOPMENT

As the nervous system develops during childhood there are some important stages that we go through.

From the age of 0 to 7 our nervous system is rapidly developing. It is learning strategies to survive in the world from our parents and people around us. We do not know if the strategies will be beneficial in the long term or how they will impact our life in the future. Unfortunately we are not consciously aware of the neurophysiological habits these strategies are creating. All we know is that the strategies being developed, and their corresponding neural pathways, are keeping us alive right now, so they are considered beneficial. This lays the foundation for our entire nervous system.

Around 7 to 9 years of age our conscious mind starts to engage and we become more aware of ourselves and things around us. We learn how to self-reflect and decide if a survival strategy is beneficial or not based on factors other than mere survival. However, we have already formed the foundation for our nervous system between the ages of 0-7 years old. So regardless of what new strategies we develop, they are potentially limited by old habits we have practiced and anchored into our nervous system between 0-7 years old.

From 7 to 25 years of age we are forming our personality. We are contemplating the meaning of life, and our understanding of "why questions." However, for most people their personality is still grounded in the survival habits of the 0-7 year old nervous system. These survival strategies are still influencing the types of ideas, goals, and future that can be accessed. Unless we have done some serious introspection and reprograming, the person we think we are and the goals we think about achieving are based on the 0-7 year old, survival-based nervous system.

Sometime between the ages of 25-35 our personality becomes crystalized in the body and we claim to know who we are and what we want from life. By the age of 35 our personal map of the world (the lens from which we gain perspective of reality) and our neural pathways are anchored in the body by glial cells. These cells wrap around our neural pathways to prevent change and make them more efficient. The body wants to maintain the patterns that have helped us survive up until this point.

Why change what is working?

A simple way to think about this is that between the ages of 0-7, 90% of the things you think and do are based on **new** information. After 35, 90% of the things you think and do are based on **old** information. It becomes increasingly more difficult to change and think about new ideas as you get older

Let's run a simple experiment to check in with the nervous system and see what is going on right now and what patterns are active in the moment.

> **EXPERIMENT: Background Noise**
>
> 1. Set a timer for 3 min.
> 2. Close your eyes. Take a slow inhale, and then exhale.
> 3. Simply notice what you notice, both internally and externally. What things are stimulating your nervous system in your current internal and external environments?
> 4. When the timer rings, open your eyes and take a moment to write down what you noticed.

During the experiment you may have become aware of pains in the body, outside stimulus, or inner mind chatter. All these things are stimulating the nervous system and triggering thoughts, feelings, and beliefs. Any stimulation of the nervous system is taking energy and focus in the moment.

By simply becoming aware of the nervous system and creating space between thought, feeling, and action, the unconscious influence it has becomes less significant. Over time, you develop the ability to bring awareness to the patterns and states that you have practiced over time, and that have been anchored in your body. When we are more in touch with ourselves we make better decisions, have better ideas, and ultimately think about new future possibilities.

THOUGHT-FEELING-ACTION-BELIEF LOOP: THE STATE OF BEING

How many thoughts does the average person have in a day? The answers vary, but studies have estimated that we have around 70,000 thoughts in day. 90% of them are from the past, and 70% of those thoughts are unconscious, and negative.

This means — and this is IMPORTANT — that you are spending most of your time thinking unconscious, negative, thoughts from the past. What types of goals do you think you will have, or what types of futures will you create, using unconscious, negative thoughts from the past?

This normal state of being is probably not an optimal state for thinking about new goals and new futures.

Consider this: every thought stimulates an electrochemical response in your neural pathways and releases hormones that create feelings in the body. As we practice these same thoughts over and over again, they not only create feelings, but they also stimulate the genes to make proteins that literally *make* your physical body. You physically become the thoughts you practice. Not just some thoughts, but every thought, becomes the building block of your physiology. The thoughts you practice over and over again become the largest building blocks.

If your thoughts are unconscious, negative, and from the past, then the body you physically create, as well as the types of goals and futures you desire, will be unconscious, negative, and from the past. But most of us want conscious, purposeful, well thought out and well *felt* out goals and futures that are positive and not limited by the past. If you agree, then keep reading.

Try this simple thought experiment. Think the thought, "Happy." As you think "Happy" what happens in your body?

You may feel more alert and pleasant. You may feel more energized and want to sit up taller. You may want to smile or you may start to recall a happy time in your life. Overall, you probably feel good…you feel happy, just from thinking "Happy."

Now try this simple experiment. Think the thought "Stressed." Notice how that thought stimulates a different feeling in the body than the thought of "Happy."

Thoughts stimulate feelings in the body. And these feelings are directly related to the neurochemical responses in the body that have been associated with that thought. As we experience life, we begin to link thoughts and feelings to specific actions, further stimulating neural pathways in the body. For example, when you think "happy" you may feel like jumping up and down, or smiling really big, or you may even become more outgoing and engaging with the people around you.

As we practice the same thoughts, feelings, and actions, we develop beliefs about the world. Again, we may believe that "happy" is a good thing, and we may believe there are experiences in life where we should be happy, like a party, and others where it is not appropriate to be happy, like a funeral. These beliefs formulate a perspective of who we think we are and how we think the world works.

As we practice this thought-feeling-action-belief loop we create a state of being in our nervous system. You may have a friend who is always happy, or someone you know who is always stressed. These are expressions of their state of being. This is a reflection of their thought-feeling-action-belief loop.

Imagine for a moment you are really hungry and you go grocery shopping. What types of things do you buy? Maybe you buy sweet things, snacks for quick energy, or

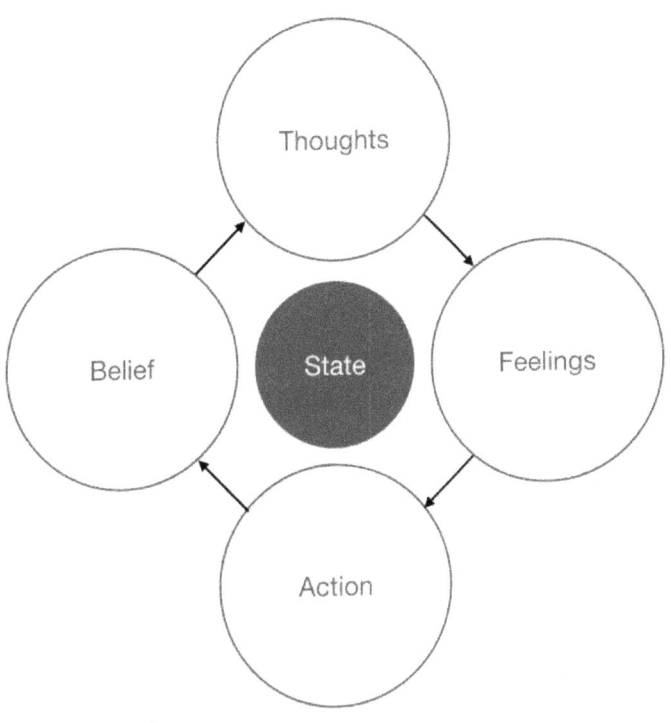

(Image 2.0) Thoughts activate feelings. Feelings inspire actions. Thoughts, feelings and actions overtime create beliefs. Beliefs influence thoughts. Thoughts, feelings, actions and beliefs create the state of being in a person.

things you do not even need. You get home and you wonder why you bought a bunch of unnecessary stuff.

Now imagine for a moment you are really satiated, maybe you just ate a big meal, and you go grocery shopping. Now what do you buy? Maybe you just purchase a drink, or just what is on your list. You probably make smarter food choices and you might even wonder why you are at the grocery store.

The idea here is that your feeling state has a big influence on the choices you make, the goals you have, and the futures you create. The world of a happy person is different than the world of a stressed person. And that happy or stressed person could be different versions of yourself. If you continue with the same thought-feeling-action-belief loop then you get the same state over and over again. Continually living in the same state puts you on a trajectory to a predetermined future, because the same thought-feeling-action-belief leads to the same results.

If you change your state, you can change your future. So what is the optimal state for thinking about your goals and the future?

COHERENT STATES

One mindset, and heart-state (as you will discover), that I have found to increase the quality of thinking and feeling, is a physiologically coherent state. Coherence is harmonious state with an increase flow of energy and coordination between different parts of a whole to allow new properties to emerge. Physiological coherence is the increased integration and flow of information and energy between the different parts of the body to allow new ideas, thoughts, goals, and future visions of the self to emerge.

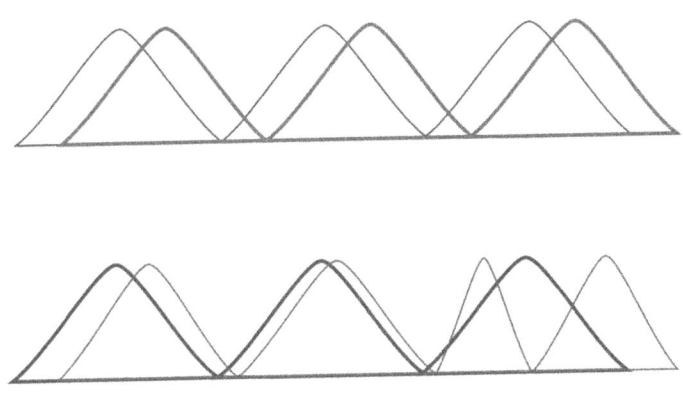

(Image 2.1) Coherent waves on the top. Incoherent waves on the bottom.

This state is characterized in the heart by healthy Heart Rate Variability (HRV). In the brain, it is characterized by an increase in alpha waves, an increase in brain wave synchrony, and an increase in neural connectivity. Seems like a good state for optimal thinking.

HRV is a measure of the time intervals between heartbeats. In general, as heart rate increases there is less time between heartbeats for variability to occur, so HRV tends to decrease. At lower heart rates there is more time between heartbeats and this typically results in an increase in HRV.

As we become more calm and relaxed we lower our heart rate and increase the HRV, resulting in a more coherent physiological state. This shifts our neurophysiological from a sympathetic (fight or flight) to a more parasympathetic (rest and digest) state.

Research by HeartMath Institute has demonstrated that when we have a more coherent HRV the body functions more efficiently, self-regulatory capacity increases, and our physiology becomes more adaptable and resilient to stress. [8]Increased HRV coherence has also been correlated with an increase in heart-brain synchrony and an increase in EEG (ElectroEncephaloGram) measured alpha activity in the brain.

When our physiology enters physiologically coherent states we have more integration and harmony in our body and we tend to feel more calm, relaxed and focused. We are more likely to get new ideas and also feel comfortable with ideas we have, even if we have never thought about them before. This is especially important as we think about new goals, new future possibilities, and the new person we are becoming. We don't want our brain to reject ideas just because they are new.

---

[8] Childre, Doc & Howard Martin, Deborah Rozman, Rollin McCraty (2016). *Heart Intelligence: Connecting with the Intuitive Guidance of the Heart*. U.S.A.: Waterfront Press

As we develop coherent states, we not only access new ideas that we have never thought about before, but we also shift our physiology from brain-centric to heart-centric. In physiologically coherent states the heart can set the rhythm for the body in four ways:

(1) Chemically through the release of hormones. For example, Oxytocin: the hormone of love, connection, and support.
(2) Neurologically through the nervous system. Specifically the Vagus Nerve which also controls are ability to be be pro-social and communicate effectively.
(3) Bio-physically through the rhythm of the heart and movement of the blood through the body.
(4) Electromagnetically through the electromagnetic field of the heart which can be measured 4-6 feet (2-3 meters) outside the body using a SQUID (Superconducting Quantum Interference Device).

As you allow the heart to set the rhythm for the body, you enter new states with new thoughts, feelings, actions, and beliefs. You increase harmony within the body and between your world and the outer world. Everything in your life starts to work more efficiently and effectively.

For example, I like to think of the heart as a conductor of an orchestra and the brain as the lead violinist. When the conductor, the heart, is in charge then all the parts of the

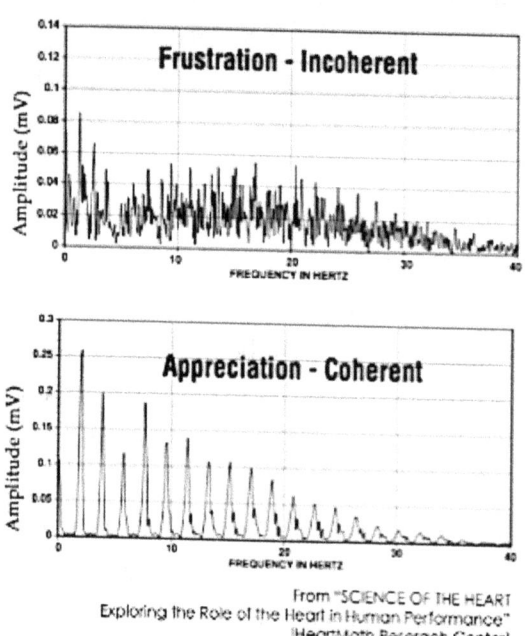

(Image 2.2) Heartmath (www.heartmath.com) has been studying how emotional states effect Heart Rate Variability (HRV). The feeling of frustration results in incoherent HRV, while the feeling of appreciation results in more coherent HRV.

orchestra play in harmony with the whole. The heart can set the context for everyone to find their place within the rhythm. When the orchestra is in rhythm together the audience enjoys the experience and everyone wins.

However, if the brain, as the lead violinist, takes over as the conductor then it may try to shine brighter, but without a clear sense for the entire orchestra. Although the lead violinist may sound amazing and steal the show, the harmony of the whole will suffer.

When the lead violinist (the brain) is following the lead of the conductor (the heart) then everything is in harmony and the entire experience is coherent.

When you enter coherent heart states you send a message to the body that you feel good. Studies have show that in negative emotional states our HRV becomes less coherent and in a positive emotional state the HRV becomes more coherent (see image 2.2). Because of feedback loops in the body as you establish a coherent HRV you send a physiological signal to the body and the brain that you are feeling good. You can then enter a calm, relaxed, and focused state for thinking about the future.

There is a simple technique you can use right now to cultivate physiological coherence. By focusing on the heart beat, your heart moves into a more coherent state. In this state stress levels decrease, the brain and heart become more integrated, cognitive function increases, and you can access more creativity. The longer you focus on the beat of the heart the more you should notice how a calm, relaxed, and focused mind state develops.

Let's run an experiment to see what physiological coherence feels like.

> **EXPERIMENT: Heart Beat Focus**
>
> 1. Set a timer for 3 min.
> 2. Close your eyes, and find your heartbeat. You may feel it on the left center of the chest, along the thumb side of the wrist, or on the front side of the neck.
> 3. As you become aware of your heartbeat, see if you can feel it grow stronger in the body and notice how it can set the rhythm for the entire body.

FEELING YOUR GOALS TO FEEL THE FUTURE

As you become more aware of your feelings, you can understand how they are influencing your state, which creates the context for thinking about ideas, goals, and the future. A coherent state creates the feeling of calm, relaxed, and focused. It is best for feeling the future. You can access this coherent state simply by sensing your heartbeat.

In a coherent state, our physiology is working in harmony, the brain and heart synchronize, and you are more in touch with how you feel and how to feel. If you can maintain a coherent state while you are thinking and feeling the future then you can access new goals and ideas about what is possible.

More importantly, you can gain a better understanding of the person you want to become in the future. As you envision the future from a coherent state, you can easily align with the feelings behind the goals. You can take note of these feelings and notice where they are missing from your life.

The language of the body is feelings. Your body must feel like taking actions to make the future a reality. When you can access positive feelings in the future, then the body is naturally drawn to take action to create the future. If you are serious about architecting the future you need to practice feeling your goals in the body. As you practice feeling your goals, you learn how to feel the future and allow that future to emerge, effortlessly.

NOTES

NOTES

CHAPTER 3 | **GOALS**

Let's think about goals for a moment and investigate what they are and how we use them in life. We tend to think of goals as an end point. However, in Old English, 'goal' originates from the related words "gal" which means obstacle or barrier, "gaelan" which means to hinder, and "geil " which refers to a passage.

A goal as the end point of a journey helps determine the end result of some effort. So you can think about goals as providing a limitation or a boundary to an activity to help you know when it has ended or some desired result has been achieved.

Imagine for a moment a soccer match without any goals. Players would run around the field and pass the ball around, steal the ball, and dribble just like they usually do. But how would you know who won the game, and what would be the point of playing the game?

Goals are important because they help us judge our ability to achieve what we set out to achieve. However, even if you do not win the game or achieve the goal, you still learn and grow in the process because playing the game changes you both physically and mentally. And this is more important than scoring a goal.

I want you to think about a goal as a vision of the future you are desiring to create, but I also want you to realize that achieving the goal does not matter. The vision that the goal helps you to understand the person you want to become. Even if you do not achieve the goal, you can still become a new person in the process.

It is not, "when you achieve the goal you will become a new person." Rather it is, "when you become a new person the goal will naturally be achieved." But when you become a new person, the goal you started with might not matter any more!

Behind every goal is a new you with a new set of feelings and a new state of being. There are new friends, new clothes, new ways of talking and walking. The cool thing is, you can learn how to embody the feelings of the goal being achieved right now and realize the future goal in the present moment through your body.

As we discussed earlier, the body does not know the difference between the past, present, or future. Take a moment and think about a past experience that fills you with joy. As you think about this past your body physically goes back into that experience. The thought of that memory stimulates similar neural pathways and releases similar hormones to recreate that experience physically in the body. Your body thinks it is really in that experience, *right now*.

We can use this same type of experimenting with thoughts and feelings about the future to bring the body into the future *as if the goal has already happened*. More importantly, you can start to build a feeling relationship with that future self who as already achieved the goal.

PERMISSION TO CHANGE

If you really want to make the changes required to become the person who can achieve your goals, then a good first step is to give yourself permission to change. Most people have never given themselves permission to change and so they do not take action to achieve the goal. It seems simple, but giving yourself permission to change and getting permission to change from others, especially those closest to you, is an important part of the process of achieving a goal.

Let's do this right now.

> **EXPERIMENT: You Have Permission To Change**
>
> 1. Stop reading or listening to this book and take a moment to say to yourself, "I have permission to change." Say it several times to yourself, and then say it out loud.
> 2. If you want to amplify this, ask someone to give you permission to change or look at yourself in the mirror and say it again with more conviction.

Notice how your physiology, and the feelings in your body, shift as you give yourself permission to change. You may feel uncomfortable, you may feel like shedding a tear, or you may feel a sense of more energy. Just notice what you notice.

THREE POWERS OF GOAL-SETTING

While developing the **Mind Lab Method** I reviewed the research on the science of goal-setting. I discovered what I will call here the three powers of goal-setting. These are important things to understand as you strive to achieve your goals and cultivate a new future self.

The Power of Writing

One of the first and most basic steps in making an idea more real is to take it from the mind and move it onto a piece of paper using the power of writing. It seems like a simple step, but do not underestimate the power of writing. When you have taken the time to write something down on paper, other people can read and understand what you are thinking, even if they are miles away.

Studies have shown that when people write their goals down they are more likely to achieve them.[9] Studies have also shown that when people write out notes by hand they had a "stronger conceptual understanding and were more successful in applying and integrating the material than those who took notes with their laptops." Writing things

---

Matthews, Gail (2015). *Goals Research Summary.* (www.dominican.edu/academics/lae/undergraduate-programs/psych/faculty/assets-gail-matthews/researchsummary2.pdf)

down engages more neural pathways, and the more neural pathways we can engage the more we start to embody the idea.

Key Point: *Thinking about our goals is not enough. Things matter more when we take the time to write them down, and they matter even more if we take the time to share them with others. Write down your goals by hand to activate the power of writing and increase the probability of a specific possibility.*

The Power of Clarity

Goals often start out being pretty vague — "make more money," "have more fun," or "spend more time with friends and family." Specificity matters: telling people to "try harder" or "do your best" is less motivating than saying, "get more than 80 percent correct," or "concentrate on beating your best time by two minutes." The specificity of the goal is important, because it helps the brain understand the what, where, when, how and why guidelines for achieving the goal.

The importance of clarity and specificity is backed by research on motivation and incentives,[10] where they

---

[10] Locke, Edwin & Gary Latham (2001). *Building a Practically Useful Theory of Goal Setting and Task Motivation: A 35-Year Odyssey.* (www.academia.edu/26293593 Toward_a_theory_of_task_motivation_and_incentives)

demonstrated that when people were given specific tasks, with measurable outcomes, they were more likely to achieve the goal.

However, clarity can be uncomfortable to the brain. By clearly stating what you want, when you want it, and how you want it, you increase the risk of failure. Failure can seem dangerous to the brain because in some situations, when you fail you are less likely to survive. Vague goals are less likely to trigger danger signs in the brain.

For example, if your goal is to "make more money," then your brain starts to look for more money. If it finds a penny, which is more money, your brain thinks, "goal achieved." Or maybe your brain thinks, "we will get more money for you, next year, or 10 years from now". Vague goals feel safe and are easier to achieve, but they do not really help us get more of what we want.

Practice stating clear goals. For example: "I want to make $10,000 in the next two weeks by getting three new business clients." The brain now has a clear idea of what needs to happen, when it needs to happen, and how it needs to happen. Remember: when we get clear on the goal then we can also get clear on the feelings behind the goal and the person we need to become to achieve it.

To reduce triggering danger signs in the brain, we can take an experimental approach to goal setting. In an experiment there is no failure and no success, only a process and results. You perform the experiment, collect the data, and then analyze the data to see what needs to be adjusted in the experiment to get more meaningful results. Then you repeat the experiment.

In the same way, as you consciously architect the future, you might not see everything clearly at first. Your job is to be as clear as you can. Then you can run an experiment, collect the data, understand what you learned in the process, and then try the experiment again. As you experiment more and more without the fear of failure or success, then you gain more clarity about what you really want and how to get it easier and faster.

Key Point: *Vague goals feel safe, but are not as productive. Practice stating clear goals to provide guidelines for your brain to make the goal a reality. Treat your goals like an experiment.*

The Power of The Future Self

The third, and final, power of goal-setting is the Power of the Future self. Consider the possibility that there is a FUTURE YOU who has already achieved all your goals and dreams. When you understand how to build a connection to that future self, you can start to embody that future now.

Keep in mind that this "future you" is not just psychologically different; rather, in the future you are also physically different. As you strive to achieve your goal you may become a person that you cannot even imagine right now. However, if you can somehow connect with that future vision of the person you are becoming, then you can start to embody and live those future thoughts, feelings, and actions in the present moment.

The reason you have a goal is because the person you are right now is not able to make the goal a part of your current reality. If you could achieve the goal right now, then it would not be a goal. For example, as I write this book, there is a future me who has already finished the book, and that person is different than the person I am right now. As I see that future vision of myself having completed the book and connect with the feelings behind that vision, my physiology begins to drive me toward that future. You are reading this book, so obviously I finished it, and I have become a different person in the process. Writing this book is no longer a goal.

Key Point: *To access the Power of the Future Self you simply need to start building a physiological relationship with that person you are in the future…right now.*

THE BARRIER TO YOUR FUTURE IS YOU

So now you might be thinking, I simply need to write down my goals with clarity and develop a relationship with my future self, and then all my goals and dreams will come true with ease.

Actually it is not that simple.

During the **Mind Lab Method** workshops people often think they need more time, more money, or more resources to make their goals real. Although these are commonly perceived barriers, the real barrier to achieving your goals is you. The person you are right now, along with the corresponding neural pathways and states of being, is designed to prevent you from making the changes required to become the future self that has already achieved the goals.

Joe Dispenza, author of *Break the Habit of Being Yourself* says that a new personality creates a new personal reality.[11] He clearly lays out the psychological and physiological challenges to creating a new personality. It is not easy to break your old habits because we are often addicted to who we think we are.

---

[11] Dispenza, Joe (2013) *Breaking The Habit of Being Yourself: How to Lose Your Mind and Create a New One.* U.S.A.: Hay House.

Bringing awareness to this problem helps us to realize that achieving a goal is not as simple as Just Do It. Most people (and most businesses) fail to achieve their goals and dreams. Look at how many people set New Year's resolutions only to discover that a month later they are back to being their "old self" again.

In the future you may need to be a drastically different than the person you are right now. These changes threaten the current state of your nervous system and seem dangerous to your brain. Your nervous systems says, "I am just fine right now being the way I am and there are no immediate threats to my survival. Why should I change?"

One of the most limiting statements you can make is, "this is just the way I am."

Change leads to uncertainty and the unknown. The primitive part of the brain thinks this will decrease the chances of survival. And in a real way, a part of you must die if you want to become a new person. Old neural pathways have to literally wither and die in order for new pathways to emerge. So, before you can even think about the goals you want to achieve you need to disengage from the physiological (neural pathways) and psychological (subconscious programs) of who you think you are.

THE TRAJECTORY TO THE FUTURE YOU: WRITE, RITE, RIGHTS OF PASSAGE

We need a process to de-couple from our current state of being and break free from the patterns in our nervous system. We also need to respect who we are right now and realize that we are becoming a new person. And we need to give ourselves permission to change.

Again, take a moment and tell yourself, "I have permission to change."

One way to think of the process of change is as a rite of passage — an experience that marks the transition from one phase of life to another. In many cultures, for example, a rite of passage is used to transition from adolescence to adulthood.

A rite of passage is typically an experience that causes a rapid change in the nervous system to allow a new person to emerge. For example, imagine a young boy, woken in the middle of the night and carried far away from the village by the men of the tribe. He is given a spear and told to survive on his own for two moons. If he survives, then upon his return to the tribe, he is considered a man.

The changes he must endure during that rite of passage are not just psychological; they are also physical and neurological. The boy had a safe, comfortable life where many things were provided for him. During the rite of passage, he was left to survive on his own. He had to find food and shelter and probably defend himself from predators. His nervous system had to rapidly adapt to match his new survival needs. When he returns, he IS a man. His entire nervous system expresses the state of being of a man.

I want you to think about goal setting as a rite of passage to your future. During the **Mind Lab Method** there are three steps to this rite of passage, (1) **write** down what you want to achieve, (2) go through the **rite** (which, as we will see, mirror the steps in the scientific method), (3) Claim your **right** to be in that future where you have achieved the goals.

Write. Rite. Right.

Many people take action towards their goals but do not achieve them simply because they don't think they have the right to achieve them. When you go through the process to purposefully feel into the future, you have the right to achieve your goals. Period.

As you journey through the writes-rites-rights of passage to a new future, it is important to maintain a coherent physiological state of feeling relaxed, calm, and focused. If your physiology does not resist the change, it can support

EXPERIMENT: Mind & Heart Goals

1. Take out a piece of paper and write down the goals you have for the next two weeks. As you think about your goals, do not filter what comes to mind, rather write down everything you think without judgement. Allow yourself to keep writing until you don't have any more goals.
2. Now set a time for 3-min and focus on your heartbeat. Close your eyes and find your heartbeat in your chest. You can put your hand on the left side of your chest to feel it. Notice how the heartbeat can grow stronger in your chest. Notice how the heartbeat moves up your neck and all the way into your brain. Notice how your heart and brain can beat in one time and one place.
3. Notice how you feel in this coherent state. Enjoy this moment and think about what matters to you most right now.
4. In this coherent state, of what matters to you most, ask yourself, "what are my goals over the next two weeks?" Ask yourself this same question two more times. Write down everything you think without judgement.

you in the process. (Remember all you have to do it take a

few minutes and sense your heartbeat to bring you back into coherence, the optimal state for thinking and feeling the future.)

FEELING YOUR GOALS

Most people are just thinking about their goals, but we also need to learn how to feel our goals. We can feel our goals in two ways: first, we can focus on the heartbeat while we think about our goals and future and see what emerges; second, we can find the feelings we will have when we achieve the goal and then activate those feelings in the body right now.

HeartScape Goals

One of the challenges with goal setting and thinking about new futures is that our physiology can shift into negative states. Fear, worry, and frustration can appear simply by thinking about the idea of making more money. To discover the best goals and futures we need to maintain coherent physiological states of relaxed, calm, and focused.

Research by the HeartMath Institute demonstrates that the heart produces more energy than the brain.[12] The heart is 80 - 100 times stronger electrically and 4,000-5,000 times stronger magnetically. Because the heart is physically more powerful than the brain, we can use it to shift our entire physiology into coherent states. We can physically move into one time, one place, and one rhythm.

As we allow the heart to take over, we can consistently communicate to the brain and body that everything is ok. Recall that the heart can communicate to the body through the rhythm of the pulse, release of hormones, stimulation of the nervous system, and the electromagnetic field. These communication pathways allow the heart to have an effect on the body that is more powerful and quicker than the brain.

By maintaining a heartbeat focus while we think about goals, we can keep our brain and body in a coherent state and allow the best goals and futures to emerge. Further, heartbeat focus increases neural integration, cognitive functioning, and heart-brain communication. In this state we have access to more possibilities and ideas that align with our entire physiology.

---

[12] McCraty, Rollin (2015) *SCIENCE OF THE HEART Exploring the Role of the Heart in Human Performance Volume 2*. U.S.A: HeartMath Institute

Goals Have Feelings

A goal is pointing you in the direction of a future where you can access feelings that have been missing in your life. When you discover the feelings behind the goal, you

realize that you can activate those feelings in your body *right now* and in some way the goal has been achieved.

We also need to realize that some goals have negative feelings behind them. If negative feelings arise as we think about a future goal, then this can provide insights into our relationship with the goal. Do you really want to achieve a goal, or even think about a goal, that has negative feelings associated with it? Your body will probably resist that future. Your body does not want to create futures where it feels bad.

If negative feelings arise when we think about a goal, we can investigate whether the feeling is based on a past experience, or if there are fears of failure or success in the future. But it can take a lot of work and effort to discover what is going on. If you continually recall the past, then you may end up repeating it.

A better strategy is to do the heartbeat focus exercise to enter a coherent state of feeling calm, relaxed, and focused. Then find the future where your goals have been achieved and find the feelings behind the achievement. Keep your focus on the positive feelings and activate them in your body, then allow your body to lead you into the future from that positive feeling state.

As you entertain the feelings behind the future goal in the present moment, then maybe the goal does not matter any more, or maybe new goals emerge. Your goals have feelings, but once you activate the feeling behind the goal, maybe the goal has already been achieved and you can move on to do something bigger and better.

For example, one Mind Lab Method participant commented on how she felt like she needed a vacation. She began to research beautiful locations, hotels and flights. She was ready to book the experience, when she realized that the process of planning the vacation, and feeling if she was already there, was enough. There was no need to take a vacation. She really just wanted the feelings.

When you learn how to feel your goals, you can accomplish more in the future than you think you can and you do not waste your time on goals that do not really matter. Later in the book you will learn a unique process to discover the feelings behind your goal. Then you will learn to use those feelings to architect the future and take action to making it a realty.

YOU HAVE TO "DATE" YOUR GOALS (OR: HOW TO SAY "I DO")

"Dating" your goals requires two things. First, you need to take the time to see what it would feel like if that goal was real. Second, you need to pick a date of completion for the goal. As you feel what it would be like for that goal to be accomplished, then you can decide if you want to have a serious relationship with that goal, or if you just want to keep it an open possibility.

As I shared the **Mind Lab Method** across the globe, one consistent aha moment for the participants was the importance of placing a date on when a goal would be completed. Not just a range of dates or a time frame, but a very specific date. This is part of the process of clarity., When you pick a date, you and your brain are clear on when this goal should be achieved. A sense of urgency for action is created.

When I challenge people to pick a date for their goals, they often struggle with the task. People like to keep it vague. It is much easier to say, "I will complete that task sometime in the next six months" than it is to say, "I am going to complete this goal on October 14, 2019". This is because picking a date of completion increases the risk of failure.

Our brains don't like failure because it is a risk to our physical and social survival. To our brain, failure can lead to physical death or social alienation. It makes us look inconsistent and untrustworthy. If we said we were going to complete goal by a specific date and it did not happen, then we feel like we are not good at following through with what we said we were going to do. This might decrease the trust we have in ourselves. It might decrease the trust that others place in us.

However, in my experience, picking a date demonstrates our commitment and focus toward the future. When we tell our brain that we are going to complete a goal on a specific date, we are sending a signal to the brain and the Reticular Activation System (RAS) that this is important for survival.

The RAS is the system in the brain that looks for things that are relevant to your mental map, and filters out things that are not relevant to your mental map. The RAS can be your best friend helping you rapidly sift through endless amounts of information to find the things most important for you to achieve your goal. By clearly stating a goal and then picking a date of completion, you are sending a strong message to the RAS to discover things that are relevant to making that goal a reality within the specified time-frame.

Now your brain will increase the energy it puts towards making the goal a reality.

At first it might seem risky to "date" your goals. You will increase the likelihood of failure, but as you continue to challenge yourself to put clear dates on goals and strive to stay accountable to the completion date, you will build a stronger sense of your own capabilities and capacity. Overtime you will become increasingly more reliable and trustworthy, both to yourself and others. You can have a better gauge on what you can achieve and how much time it will take. As a result you are less likely to overcommit, quit during the process, or even underestimate what you can accomplish.

But before you pick a date of completion, you must take some time to "date" your goals. By "dating" your goals you can see how they would feel if they were accomplished. You start to build a physiological relationship with them to see if they are something you want to get serious about.

When you go on your first date, it does not always feel comfortable, but that does not mean that there is no long-term potential. Trying new things is typically uncomfortable to the brain and body. As you go on more and more dates with the person (or your goals), you can start to build more comfort with them and make a better decision about whether there is an opportunity to "get serious."

Just like dating people, it is a good practice to date your goals. If you do not feel good about the goal during the dating process, then you can easily drop it and find a goal that is more aligned with your future.

If you discover the goal has long-term potential, then "dating" it by picking a specific date of completion and saying "I do," will increase the probability that it will become a reality.

SHOW UP NO MATTER WHAT

Once you have set your goals and are committed to a future, you have to start showing up for that goal and that future 100%. No matter what.

While hosting the **Mind Lab Method** down the West Coast of the US, we began to build momentum around the idea. We hosted our first 50+ person event in Venice Beach, California with rave reviews. We were ready for this Mind Lab experiment to blow up!

The following week we showed up for an event at a co-working space in Santa Monica and only one person attended.

There was a moment in my mind where I thought to cancel the event. We had just hosted a 50+ person workshop with a lot of great energy and excitement, and now we had to host an event with one person. It felt like our progress was moving in reverse.

However, I realized this was a great opportunity to show up 100% for the event no matter how many people attended. Give 100% to the future that we were creating and commit to do the event even if only one person attended.

We walked this one attendee through the entire Mind Lab Experiment and by the end her mind was blown! She had such a great experience. Realizing how valuable the Mind Lab was for entrepreneurs, she confessed that she was the general manager of several co-working locations in the greater Los Angeles area. She said, "the next event I will have it packed for you".

A few months later, as I continued sharing the **Mind Lab Method** throughout Asia. An event Chiang Mai, Thailand was promoted for just ten days and I was 100% commitment to hosting the event regardless if anyone showed up or not. As I walked into the event space on the day of the event the room was buzzing with excitement and over 125 people were in attendance.

Whether there is one person in the room or one hundred people, I have learned to give one hundred percent to the future I want.

RICE COOKER FUTURES

Before developing the **Mind Lab Method**, goal setting always seemed like hard work. Many goal setting processes require you to measure metrics of change every day. It reminds me of the old saying, "a watched pot won't boil."

I like to create what I call rice cooker futures. Just like a rice cooker, you throw in all the ingredients and then you close the top. The rice cooker will let you know when the rice is finished. You set it and forget it. No need to watch or wait.

How do you set your goal and forget it?

The **Mind Lab Method** will walk you through a series of experiments to align your heart, brain, & body with your future and then anchor that future into your physiology as if it has already happened. The process culminates with the creation of a timeline of their future with completion dates for their goals.

Goal setting is not just writing down a To Do list. It is a process of changing your entire physiology through practice, commitment, and transformation. As you think about the future and write down what you want, you need to continually maintain the feeling as if it has already happened. Creating a timeline and a date of completion for the goals is like closing the lid on the rice cooker of your future. By then, you can sit back and allow the process to unfold.

Once you have anchored the goal with a future date of completion, your brain, heart & body know exactly what to do to take action without resistance. There is no need to record daily metrics or constantly stay focused on the goal (though you can do these things if you want).

When I do the **Mind Lab Method** for myself, I like to go through the five steps and set the timeline, and then forget it. I put all the ingredients in the rice cooker of my future and see how it turns out. If it does not go as planned, then I recalibrate and repeat. If things go as planned, great! And often, when I set it and forget it, the future results are even better than I imagined.

So if you are willing to take the time to go through the process of architecting a well thought out and felt out purposeful future (ingredients), with a specific date of completion (timer), then just like a rice cooker, your future will be waiting for you when you are ready.

In the next chapter you will learn the 5-step process for creating a rice cooker future.

Are you ready?

NOTES

NOTES

NOTES

NOTE: The original ideas for the tools in Chapter 4 and the experiments in Chapter 5 of this book were sprouted in collaboration with Jonathan Fritzler, when we were co-hosting *Mind Lab: This is an Experiment* Events in 2015.

I encourage you to check out his current work at:
www.jonathanfritzler.org
www.mindlab.institute

*Your Goals and the Future
Are An Experiment*

CHAPTER 4 | **THE FIVE STEPS OF THE MIND LAB METHOD**

The **Mind Lab Method** has been developed over years of continual testing with live audiences throughout the world. After each experience, feedback was gathered and the process was optimized to ensure maximal results with the least amount of effort.

In this chapter I share a simple five step process that you can practice and repeat to achieve your goals with ease. If you are new to goal setting then this is a great place to start. On the other hand, if you are a veteran goal achiever you will learn some new techniques to achieve your goals faster and with less effort.

Remember, this is yoga for the mind. You don't do handstands on the first day. You have to learn, practice, experiment and repeat.

THE SCIENCE OF GOAL SETTING

The scientific method is a powerful process that has allowed us to consistently change the fundamental understanding of reality. For example, the scientific method has turned a flat earth into a round earth and has transformed the solar system from geocentric (earth centered) to heliocentric (sun centered). Most of our understanding of the universe and how it works has gone through the rigors of the scientific method to transform chaos and uncertainty into order and certainty.

What if we used that same thinking to create our future and achieve our goals?

The steps of the scientific method we will use are (1) Ask a Question, (2) Background Research, (3) Create Hypothesis, (4) Test Hypothesis, (5) Draw a Conclusion.

As we follow the scientific method as a process for personal transformation, let me remind you that it is just an experiment. There is no success or failure in science. Rather there is a hypothesis (an idea to test) and experiment results. Regardless of the result we get new information and insights that can be used to reformulate the hypothesis about our future. Repeating the process helps us fine-tune our ability to develop goals that align with and stretch our capacity and capabilities.

THE MIND LAB METHOD (FULL VERSION)

The full **Mind Lab Method** will give you new tools and perspectives to enhance your ability to architect your future. Remember: Practice, practice, practice.

STEP 1: ASK A QUESTION ABOUT YOUR FUTURE

Every experiment starts with a question. Asking a question decouples the brain from what is known so new ideas can emerge. For example, instead of knowing what your goals are and writing them down, what if you took a moment to ask the question, "what are my goals in the next three months?" and then observe what new insights arise.

As we feel the future of our goals we are looking for answers that are a little uncomfortable and that we have never thought about before. These answers are novel and not based on the past nervous system or childhood patterns. This is what makes us feel uncomfortable about them.

Answers that feel comfortable, or that we have thought about before, are based on the past. To access the future self that is free from past limitations, you need to learn how to discover goals that require change and growth. Remember it is the job of the brain and the current self to prevent change. The task of finding uncomfortable and unknown goals is not easy.

One question I asked myself while I was in my second year of medical school was, "what happens if I reached my goal of retirement, right now?" That type of question resulted in some very interesting and uncomfortable answers that I had never thought about before. For example, one answer I got was, "you can move to Hawai'i and learn how to surf." I ended up experimenting with that answer and it has put me on an amazing future trajectory that I never expected.

During live Mind Lab Method events, people partner up and ask a question about their partner, something that they cannot possibly know the answer to. The purpose is to develop the skill of asking questions and allowing our mind to make up the answers. This experiment also exercises the imaginative part of the brain, which is often dormant.

Typically when we think about the future the part of the brain associated with recalling the past gets activated, and then we use the past to create the future. However, if we want to find answers that are not limited by the past, then we need to activate the part of the brain that is associated with imagination. We need to practice making things up.

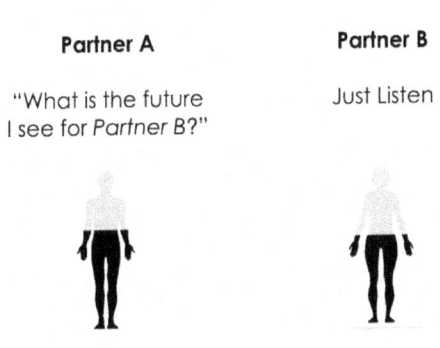

For the experiment one person is partner A and the other is partner B. Partner A starts by asking the question "what is the future I see for this person (partner B)." After Partner A asks the question, then Partner A proceeds to answer the question.

Yes, you read that correctly. Partner A asks the question and then answers the question. The job of partner B is to sit and listen.

When you ask a question the brain will look for answers. Typically the brain wants to get the answer right, but there is no right answer in this experiment. There is no wrong answer either. You just have to make something up.

EXPERIMENT: HeartScape

1. Set a timer for three minutes. Close your eyes, and find your heartbeat. You may feel it on the left center of the chest, along the thumb side of the wrist or in the neck. As you become aware of your heartbeat, see if you can feel it grow stronger. See if you can feel your heart beat all the way into the brain and notice how your brain and heart can be in one time, one place, and one rhythm.
2. Now set a timer for five to ten minutes and perform a HeartScape of the question, "what do I want to accomplish in the next three months." Keep your focus on your heartbeat while you ask the question and write down whatever ideas about the future come to mind.
3. This is a free write, so challenge yourself to write as much as possible. As you run out of ideas go back to focus on the heartbeat and then ask the question again.

You can try this right now. Find a friend or a random person and ask them if they would like to do an experiment with you. Tell them you are going to share your thoughts on their future. Ask yourself the question, "what is the future I see for this person," and then share whatever comes to mind. Do not filter the answers, just share the images, thoughts, feelings, and words as they arise.

During this experiment people sometimes feel uncomfortable and nervous. They may not be comfortable with making things up, they may try to get the right answer, or fear getting the wrong answer. Sometimes people freeze or break into a sweat. This is all information about how our nervous system is responding to the task of making things up.

After the experiment I ask the participants what they learned. Typically the results are the following.

1) When you ask a question your brain will make up answers and some of those answers turn out to be accurate.
2) If you just start talking, then more answers start to arise. If you reward your brain for sharing what it is making up then it will make up more and more.
3) People often make up better and more positive futures for other people than they do for themselves (keep this in mind when you make up your own future).
4) It feels good to make up the future. Exploring your imagination is fun.

Mind Dump: Ask a Question With Your Brain

Now that you understand how to ask questions and allow answers to emerge using the imagination, let's apply this same process to your goals. Instead of thinking that you know what your goals are, I want you to ask the question about your goals and allow new ideas and even uncomfortable ideas to emerge.

We will ask the question about our future using a three month timeframe. Why three-months? First, three months is a season. This aligns your future timeline with the seasons of life. Second, a lot can happen in three months, more than you can imagine, when you use the Mind Lab Method tools and techniques. And third, it is not too far into the future, so the brain takes it seriously.

So ask yourself the question, "what do I want to accomplish in the next three months." When you ask the question, answers will come to mind and then you can harvest the answers by writing them down.

Writing down your ideas about your future goals when you ask the question is called a Mind Dump. It serves a couple purposes: (1) to see what is in our mind when we ask the question about our goals over the next 3-months and (2) it helps to clear the mind of old ideas that we have not taken action on and reduces cognitive overload.

When you perform the Mind Dump there are few things to consider. First, write down anything that comes to mind, without judgement. You are not trying to find the right answer, rather you are investigating what is in the brain when you ask the question. If it seems like a goal that is too small, too big, or just silly, you still write it down. Second, challenge yourself to write for at least five minutes. When you seem to run out of answers, ask the question again. You might be surprised by what ideas emerge at the last minute.

Let's see what new futures we can discover when we take the first step in the Mind Lab Method and ask a question.

HeartScape: Ask a Question Coherently, From the Heart

Now we are going to ask the same question about our future, but we are going to do it in a different state. Remember, when you change your state you change the types of ideas, goals, and futures you think about. As you enter a coherent physiological state your brain and heart synchronize, you increase cognitive function, neural integration, and creativity, while also decreasing stress. This puts you in a calm, relaxed and focused state for discovering new insights about yourself and the future.

We will use the simple technique of heartbeat focus to cultivate a coherent state.

The final step in the HeartScape is to pick a theme for the next three months of your life or business. Think of this theme as a chapter in a book of your life. This theme will help you select the goals that are more aligned with your future. As you focus on the heartbeat ask yourself what is the theme of the next three months. Then write it down.

STEP 2: BACKGROUND RESEARCH

The second step in the scientific method is Background Research. During this step, scientists investigate previous research that has been performed concerning the key question. During the **Mind Lab Method** we do background research in the subconscious mind to see what we are thinking and feeling about the goals we have written down during the Mind Dump and HeartScape.

To access the subconscious mind you will do a guided visualization/micro-meditation to connect with your past and future self. In this meditation you will be guided through a process of forgiving the past self and connecting with the future self. Forgiveness is associated with positive changes in the brain and increase emotional regulation.[13]

At any point during the meditation if you gain new insights you can take a moment, exist the meditation, and write them down. Then go back into the meditation and continue. Remember we are doing research in our subconscious to see what is there, without judgment or

---

[13] Emiliano Ricciardi, Giuseppina Rota, Lorenzo Sani, Claudio Gentili, Anna Gaglianese, Mario Guazzelli, and Pietro Pietrini. How the brain heals emotional wounds: the functional neuroanatomy of forgiveness. Front Hum Neurosci. 2013; 7: 839.

expectation. Trust the process and just notice what you notice.

Past and Future Self Meditation

- Close your eyes and take three slow, deep breaths.
- Find your heartbeat and notice how your heartbeat moves up your neck and into your brain.
- Bring awareness back to the heartbeat in the chest.
- Notice a spiral of DNA expanding from your heart backwards in space and time
- Realize that the spiral of DNA has all your life stories and experiences.
- Allow your mind to move along that spiral of DNA backwards in space and time.
- As you move backwards in space in time, notice any places that feel sticky or stuck. Send in love and forgiveness to those places and smooth them out.
- Continue to move backwards in space and time along that spiral of DNA and continue to smooth it out.
- Allow your mind to arrive at the day you are born and connect with the heartbeat of that newborn child that is you.
- Take a deep, slow inhale. And exhale.
- Thank yourself for being born. And realize all the potential you have and the unlimited possibilities available to you.
- Now allow your mind to move forward in space and time along the spiral of DNA. Notice how much smoother and clearer it is now.
- Arrive at the present moment. Take an inhale, and exhale.

- Now allow your mind to move forward in space in time along the future timeline of your life.
- Allow your mind to arrive at a nice, clean, crisp forest.
- Walk around the forest and notice how it feels in your body. Notice any sounds, smells and sights. Bring your body fully into the experience.
- As you walk through the forest you notice a house and a porch with two chairs.
- As you get closer you realize that in one chair is an old man or an old woman. And you realize that that old man or old woman is you. The future you.
- Sit down next to the future you and look yourself in the eyes.
- Notice how you look in the future. How does your hair look, what clothes are you wearing, what does your face look like? Notice what you notice.
- Now look yourself in the eyes, and ask yourself, "What do I need to know right now?"
- Take note of whatever you hear.
- Again ask yourself, "What do I need to know right now?"
- And a third time, ask yourself, "What do I need to know right now?"
- Now your future self has a gift for you. Allow your future self to hand you the gift and when you are ready, open it up to see what it is. Accept the gift without judgement.
- Look your future self in the eyes and thank yourself.
- Now allow your mind to move backwards in space and time to the present moment.
- Take a slow, deep inhale. Exhale.
- Open your eyes when you are ready.

Take note of any new insights or ideas. Also, realize that any new images or feelings are actually changing your physiology and aligning you with your goals. When you bring awareness to things, your brain changes and grows. This simple experiment and meditation has either helped you increase the probability of achieving your goals or it has helped you gain some more clarity about what is holding you back from achieving your goals. Maybe it did both!

You are now ready to pick your top three goals and gain more clarity about the future.

Select Your Top Three Goals

It is time to gain clarity by selecting the top three goals you want to achieve over the next three months. Yes, you can achieve all your goals, but you have to be clear about which ones are most important right now. After you complete your top three goals you can move on to other goals.

Look at your notes from the Mind Dump, HeartScape and Theme to select the top three goals that you want to accomplish over the next three months. Here are some things to keep in mind during this part of the process:

1. Keep yourself in a calm, relaxed, and focused state while selecting your goals. You can focus on the heartbeat to enter this state.
2. Pick three goals: no more, and no less. This is a practice of clarity. If you feel like there are more than three goals that need to be accomplished in the next three months, that is great. But for now, just pick your top three goals. You can complete them first and then move on to more goals in the future.
3. Some of your goals may actually be one big goal. See if you can combine some of your goals together.
4. Some of your goals may not be very specific. That is okay, just start with what you have.
5. Some of your goals may feel like they are too audacious to be completed in three months. If that is case you can choose a different goal, or experiment with the idea that you might be able to accomplish more than you think you can in three months. It happens all the time.
6. Now select your top three goals and write them down.

My THEME for the next 3-months is...

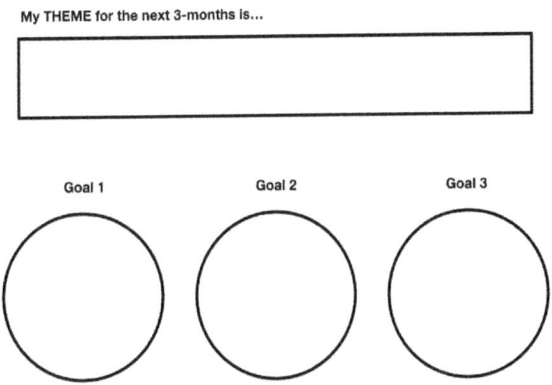

STEP 3: CREATE HYPOTHESIS

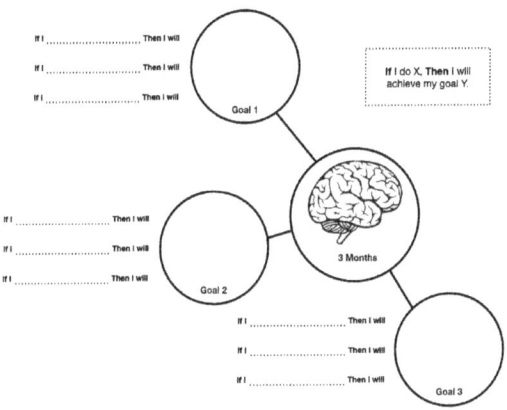

The third step in the scientific method is Create a Hypothesis. A hypothesis is an "If/Then" statement that helps guide the experiment. Basically you are stating, If I do X, then I assume that Y will happen. For example, if I exercise 30 minutes every day, then I will get in better physical shape. Now you have a testable statement from which to move forward with the experiment.

Let's get back to our top three goals and explore them using a Mind Map. Create a Mind Map like the image above and write your top three goals in the circles. The Mind Map is a way to look at your goals from a new perspective and see how they interconnect to create an integrated future. When we can see a future where all the things we want to accomplish are connected, then it is easier for the brain to focus on making that future a reality.

Using the goals in your Mind Map you can create a hypothesis about how these goals could be achieved. For example, if I want to become a better singer, then my hypothesis could be, "If I sing in the shower every morning, then I will become a better singer" or "If I take singing lessons, then I will become a better singer."

However, as we explore "If/Then" statements, our brain is often limited in its thinking. For example, if one of your goals is an all-expense-paid trip to Hawai'i, your brain will immediately think of all the reasons why that cannot happen: you have to work, no one would pay for you to go there, or maybe you have children with no one to watch and care for them if you went on a vacation.

While creating a hypothesis we want to ignore the barriers and only look at avenues to the future where the goal is achieved. The more ways we can see a pathway to the future, the more likely we are to find the best way to get there that aligns with your brain, heart, & body.

Take a moment and ask yourself, "how could I get an all-expense-paid trip to Hawai'i?" If you allow new ideas to arise you might realize that a friend could invite you for an all-expense-paid trip to Hawai'i. Your work could send you to Hawai'i. You could go to a local store that is having a sweepstakes for an all-expense-paid trip to Hawai'i and you could win it. And so on. When you allow yourself to be creative you will realize that there are a million ways something could happen.

When your mind says, "that cannot happen," take another approach and ask yourself, "how could it happen?"

Typically the "If/Then" statement is limited by the past and we need to challenge our thinking to get creative with pathways to the future. If my goal is to make $10,000 more dollars in one month, my brain might initially think about my past experience making money, and use the same logic to develop the "If/Then" statement for the future. If in the past my pathway to more money was working for an hourly wage, then I might create an "If/Then" statement based on the idea, "if I work more hours, then I will make more money."

However, if I allow myself to get creative and break from from the logic of the past I could imagine many other ways that $10,000 could appear. For example, I could get a random check in the mail for $10,000; I could buy a lottery ticket that wins me $10,000; I could be gifted a car that I then sell for $10,000; a friend of mine could sell his company for millions of dollars and gift me $10,000; and so on. If you allow yourself to be creative you will realize there are many possible "If/Then" statements that could allow you to achieve your goal.

> **EXPERIMENT: If, Then**
>
> 1. Take a few minutes and write down ways in which each goal could happen in the format of "If I do X, Then the goal Y will happen."
> 2. Start by focusing on the heartbeat to enter a calm, relaxed, and focused state. Be creative and explore pathways to the goal that you have never thought about before. Use the same type of thinking that you used in the Ask a Question experiment.
> 3. Start with, "what could I do to achieve goal X?" Then write down whatever comes to mind, even if it seems ridiculous.

If you want to amplify the If/Then experiment, then find someone and ask them to think of ways in which your goal could be achieved. This person, especially if they are a stranger, does not have the same limiting beliefs or strategies that you might have. Because they are not limited by your past they can offer new perspective on what "If/Then" statements are possible.

STEP 4: TEST HYPOTHESIS

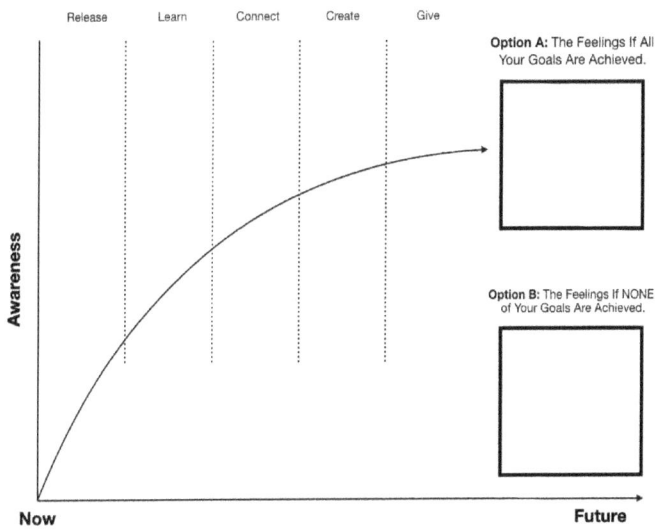

At this point in the process you should have gained clarity about your goals and developed hypothesis (If/Then statements) about how you might achieve them. Now you want to test the hypothesis you have developed and explore trajectories to specific futures. This is where you practice *feeling the future*.

In Hawai'i there is an island called Kaho'olawe. It was an island for navigation and navigation training. On the highest peak of the island a navigator would sit and point ships in the right direction to give them the best possible start. The Hawaiians knew that if the ship was off just a little as it set sail on a long journey, then they could miss the target by a lot. You need to give yourself the best possible start as you move on a new future trajectory.

Even with a good start you may need to pivot along the path to the goals. Every time your mindset changes, or when you reach a goal, your direction can change. Small shifts in your awareness and focus can have huge impacts on the result of the trajectory. The goal is a vision of who you are becoming and can be used as a focal point in the future to maintain your trajectory.

One of the best ways to keep that focus is to connect with the feelings you are trying to create in your body by achieving the goal. The reality is that we are not really interested in achieving the goal; we are really after the feeling that the goal will bring when we achieve it. When we learn how to feel the feelings right now in the body, then the goal is not as important. We can enter a new state from which to decide if we really want to achieve the goal or not. Maybe we just want to feel the future of a particular goal so we can enter the right state to discover what we really want from life.

The key point here is that it is not, "when I achieve the goal, I will feel this way." Rather it is, "when I feel this way, I will achieve the goal." For example, maybe you want to be in a relationship because it will make you feel loved. But if you do not feel loved right now, do you think you will be able to get a loving relationship? Maybe you want to be the boss so you will feel more confident and powerful. But if you do not feel confident and powerful, do you think you can become the boss?

If you really want to achieve your goals fast, then feel the feelings of the goal being achieved in your body right now. Embody the future person you want to become, and then realize that from this new physiological state the goal is more likely to be achieved.

Feeling the Future Trajectory

Let's get to work plotting a trajectory into our future where you have become the person who has achieved the goals you desire.

Here are the steps (see the trajectory image at the start of the section):
1. In the Box Labeled Option A write down how you will feel when you achieve your top three goals. Write those feelings in the box.
2. In the Box Labeled Option B write down how you will feel if you do not achieve your top three goals. Write those feelings in the box.
3. These are two potential future extremes that you can plot a course towards. In one future, Option A, you become

the person that can achieve all your goals and dreams. In the other, option B, none of your goals and dreams become real. Notice that there are also a lot of options in between these two.

4. You want to plot the course, and stay on the course, towards Option A. To do that you need to keep our level of conscious awareness high.
5. Now draw a line from the NOW point on the bottom left of the page to Option A. This is your path to the future you want.
6. To increase awareness on how you can stay on that course, ask yourself the questions in each column and write down a few answers to each in the specified columns.
7. Remember, these questions are no longer goal focused, rather they are feeling-focused. They help us understand that there are things we can do right now to cultivate the feelings we want regardless if we achieve the goal or not.
8. Questions to ask yourself: write down three to five answers for each question
    8.1. What do I need to **release** to feel option A?
    8.2. What do I need to **learn** to feel option A?
    8.3. What do I need to **create** to feel option A?
    8.4. Who or what do I need to **connect** with to feel option A?
    8.5. What do I need to **give** to feel option A?
9. Review your answers and select one from each column that you feel matters the most.

10. Take a moment and fill out the sentence at the bottom of the page using the answers. I am releasing _____,

learning _____, connecting with _____, creating _____, and giving_____ so I can feel like _____ *(Option A)*.

11. Read the statement several times to yourself and out loud. Notice how the sentence feels when you say it. Notice if you are confident or hesitant about the words. This is a good test to see if you are ready to move into that future and the feelings it will bring.
12. If you want to amplify the experiment, read the statement out loud to someone else and have then give you feedback on how it felt to them as you read it. Were you able to share your trajectory with clarity and confidence?

Commit to Your Future Self

It is time for a check in. We are about to move into the final step of the **Mind Lab Method** and you need to be ready for this.

Ask yourself right now, "Am I 100% committed to creating my future?" Notice how you feel about the question. You need to be 100% ready to do this. Because once you do the final step there is no turning back.

Are you ready?

Seriously, are you ready? Are you going to do this next step with 100% commitment and focus? Or are going to do what most people normally do and say you are going to take action towards achieving your goals, but not actually take the action?

Close your eyes and say to yourself, "I am ready." Repeat it again and again until you really feel ready to commit to cultivating a new future self.

When you are ready, then you are welcome to do the final step.

STEP 5: DRAW A CONCLUSION

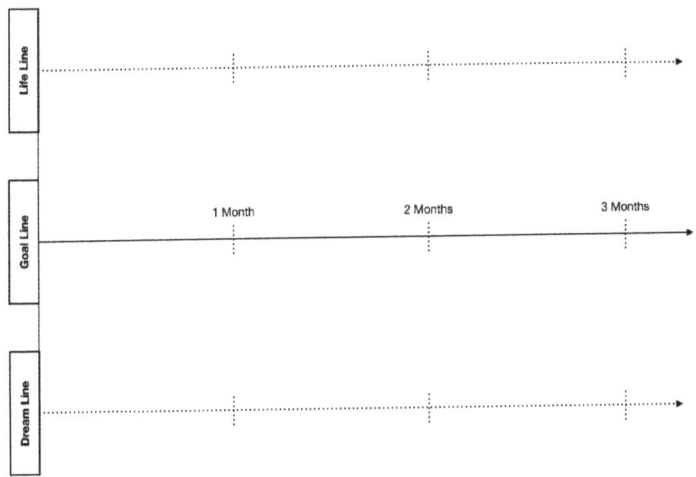

We are now ready for the final step in the science of goal-setting, Draw a Conclusion. This is where you really architect your future. Let's review the process so far: you have asked a question about the future to discover new goals, performed background research in the mind to reveal new insights about your goals, developed a hypothesis about the pathway to achieve your goals and tested the hypothesis using the power of feeling the future. Now it is time to architect your future using timelines.

Building a timeline of when you want your goals to happen adds another layer of clarity and specificity to the goal-setting process. We don't actually know what is really going to happen in the future, or over the next three months, because it has not happened yet. However, we can clearly state what we want to happen and when we want it to happen and develop a level of certainty about the future to make it matter in the present moment.

Remember, this is just an experiment and there is no failure or success, only information. This is important, because you may have goals that you do not know when they are going to happen or that you feel like you do not have full control over making happen. This does not mean that you cannot state when we want it to happen and see how accurate you can get with your prediction.

We are just making up the future, so make up a date when your goal will become a reality.

The timeline helps to organize the data from the past experiments into one visual framework. We are thinking logically about actionable steps towards our goals, but we are also thinking creatively and using a visual experience to anchor our strategy in the subconscious mind.

With a timeline of the future, the brain's Reticular Activation System (RAS) is now attuned to things that will help make that goal a reality in the specified timeframe. Deadlines tell the brain that there is a sense of urgency and that the goal is important for survival. Without a timeframe then the brain does not take the goal seriously and focuses on more urgent matters.

Preparing for Timeline Design

You will need about 15-30 minutes to create a good timeline. Find a comfortable, quiet space where you can focus and be aware of your state.

Check in to ensure that your heart and brain are coherent. You can do a short heartbeat focus before and during the process to maintain a coherent state; feeling relaxed, calm and focused.

As you develop your timeline notice if specific goals change your state and make you feel uncomfortable and stressed. This provides you some insight into the physiological relationship to the goal and whether you feel ready to accomplish it in the timeframe specified.

Timeline Design

On your timeline sheet you will see three lines: The Life Line, Goal Line, and Dream Line. You will also notice three months of time.

The first thing you will do is write down the dates for the three months you will be including on your timeline.

The Life Line (20%)

The Life Line section is for recording what's already planned for your life or business. These are not goals, rather they are important events in your life that are 80-90% confirmed. They could be related to school, work, vacation times, meetings, breaks in your schedule or availability.

Take a few minutes and write down all the things that are already planned to happen over the next three months on the Life Line. Make sure that the event dates align within the correct timeframe. Even if you have these dates listed on a digital calendar it is good to use the power of writing to activate them the subconscious. Further, creating a timeline helps to integrate the future into one clear vision within the brain.

The Life Line is also important because it helps is see where our goals can align with your life. If one of our goals is to take a vacation to Hawaii, then we need to know what is already planned so the dates do not conflict.

Goal Line (60%)

On the Goal Line you will write down your top three goals. The important thing is to pick the date or timeframe in which the goal will be accomplished.

Some people are hesitant to pick dates because they fear things will not happen as they plan and they will be a failure. Recall this is an experiment. If it does not happen then you pivot and re-adjust and bring awareness to why it did not happen. You learn and try again.

Picking a date is important because it encourages the subconscious mind to make the goal happen by the specified date and activates the brain's RAS to look for things that will support you in achieving the goal.

Take a moment and pick the dates by which each of your top three goals will be completed and write them on the goal line.

Additional things to add to the goal line.

A. You can refer back to the Mind Map to identify actions that you can take toward your goals. The Mind Map should provide you with some strategies to make the idea a reality. You can list some milestones associated with those strategies that lead to the goal.

B. The trajectory sheet can provide you with a vision for staying in alignment with your desired future. List the thing you need to release, learn, create, and give to feel Option A. Pick the date when those things are going to happen.

Dream Line (20%)

On the Dream Line you will write down your breakthroughs and miracles. This is an opportunity to dream big, be creative, and have fun with the future.

Start by picking a financial goal that is just outside your realm of possibility, something that would really surprise you. Then pick a few other big dreams that you could imagine happening over the next three months. Again, pick a date for each one of these dreams to occur.

We have had people write down miracles on the Dream Line and they have come true. For example, one person called us up two weeks after a Mind Lab event to share that something he wrote down on the dream line came true even though he had no control over making it happen. Somehow gaining clarity and specifying a date increased the probability of the miracle becoming a reality.

Storing Your Timeline

After completing the timeline you can choose to keep it with you and use it as a map to the future, or you can just store it away until the three months is up.

At the end of the three months you can look back at the timeline and see how your experiment ended up. Whatever happened is feedback and information for you to use in the next experiment with your future. Remember, no expectations, just experimentation.

For me the process of crafting a timeline helps me develop a Rice Cooker Future. You put in the ingredients of the **Mind Lab Method** and then close the lid and set a timeline. When the rice is done the cooker stops and it even keeps the rice warm for you. There is no need to worry about it. You set it and forget it.

When you timeline out the future the same thing happens. You put all the ingredients into your future, and then you set it and forget it. You come back to take a look when it is all done.

CLOSING REFLECTION

After completing your timeline it is important to take a moment and reflect on the goal-setting process. You have done some purposeful thinking and feeling and now is a good time to reflect on how you, your brain, and your future have already changed just by going through the process.

Reflection steps.
1. Take three slow, deep inhales and exhales.
2. Connect with your heartbeat.
3. Thank yourself for taking the time to strategize your goals and plan your future.
4. See yourself moving into the future free from the past, the old self gracefully falling away as you step into your new self.
5. Say a prayer in your own way over the next three months of your life.
6. Realize you did the work, you have the right to achieve your goals and you are ready
7. Realize that this is all just an experiment and with no expectations you move into the future.
8. Feel the future as if it has already happened.
9. Take a big inhale. Exhale. Then let it all go.

NOTES

THE MIND LAB METHOD
(SIMPLIFIED VERSION)

In the next few pages you will find a quick summary of the steps in the Full Version. As you continue to practice these steps, you should notice how your accuracy in creating the future increases.

Before You start:
- Grab a pen and paper
- Remove all distractions
- Tell Yourself You have Permission to change
- Give 100%

Step 1
Ask a Question (With the Brain and Heart)

1. Mind Dump: Ask yourself, "what do I want to accomplish in the next three months." As you ask the question do a Mind Dump of every answer that comes to mind. Write as much as you can without thinking.
2. HeartScape: Now, connect with your heartbeat by focusing on the beat and rhythm of your heart for three minutes. Then ask yourself the question again, "what do I want to accomplish in the next three months." Do a HeartScape of all the answers that come to mind. Free-write (write as much as you can) for three minutes.
3. Again, find the beat of your heart and ask yourself, "what is the theme of my life (or business) over the next three months. This theme is the overarching feeling, like a title of a book chapter.

My THEME for the next 3-months is...

[   ]

Goal 1   Goal 2   Goal 3

( )   ( )   ( )

Step 2
Background Research (In The Subconscious)

1. Look at the goals you wrote down. Do a meditation on the stories and experiences of the past before you go into the future and meet your future self. This meditation is explained in the experiment section.
2. When you meet your future self in the meditation ask, "what do I need to know right now?" Accept whatever answer arises.
3. After doing background research in your mind, look back at your Mind Dump and HeartScape results. Do a 1min heart beat focus and select the top three goals you would like to achieve in the next three months. Picking three goals brings more clarity to the future.

Step 3
Create Hypothesis (If, Then Statements)

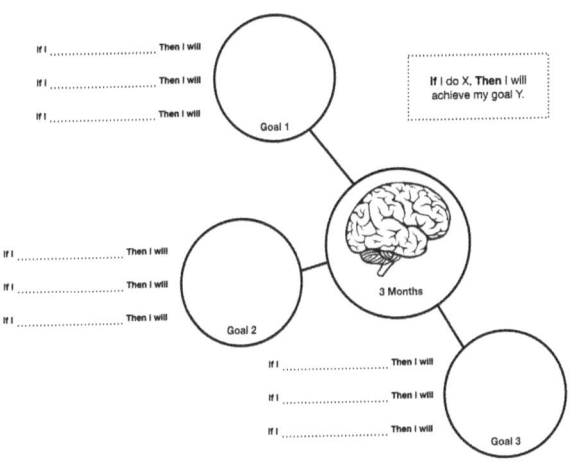

1. Activate the power of writing by making a Mind Map of your goals.
2. Consider several ways in which each goal could become a reality. Think, If I do X, Then this goal will happen. Challenge yourself to get creative with pathways to your goal. Even things that sound ridiculous might provide unique insights to your future trajectory.

Step 4

Test Hypothesis (Trajectory to the Future)

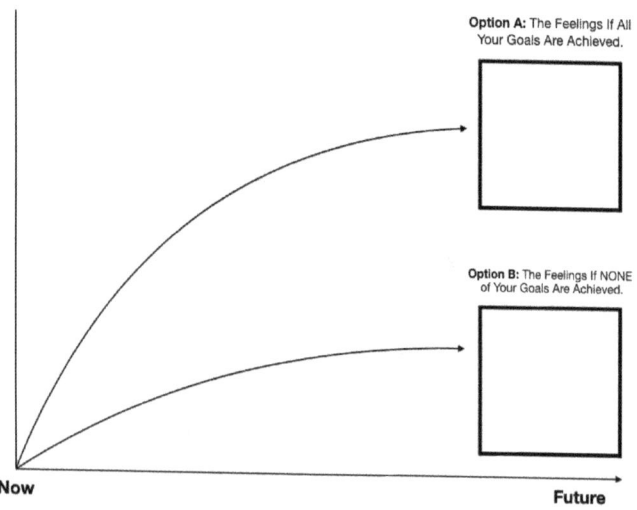

1. Imagine the future in which all your goals are achieved. Note the feelings of achieving the goal in the box labeled Option A.
2. Now imagine the future in which none of your goals become real. Note the feelings in the box labeled Option B.
3. Recall that Option A and Option B are the two extremes of the future. In one future all your goals are realized. In the other, none of your goals are realized. There is a lot of space in between.

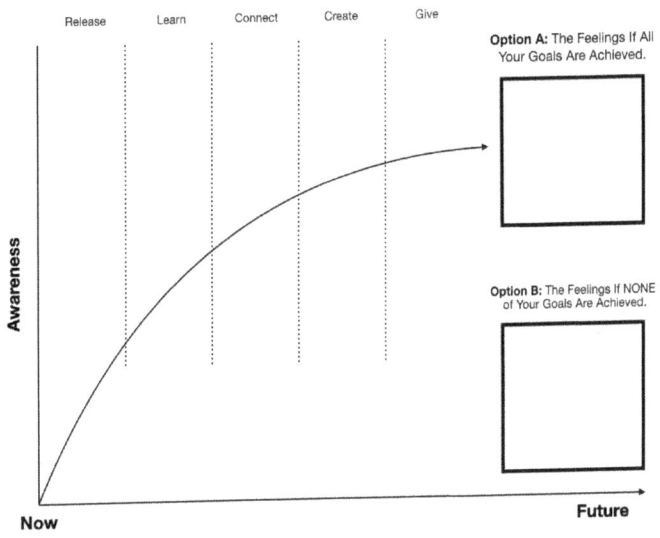

4. Following the diagram, write down things that you will release, learn, connect with, create, and give that will help you feel option A in the column as labeled.
5. Select one answer from each column.
6. Take a moment and write out the following statement using the answers. "I am releasing _____, learning _____, connecting with _____, create _____, and giving _____ so I can feel like option A (*write down the feelings*)."
7. Now read this statement to yourself at least three times silently, and then three times aloud to align your thoughts and feelings to that future trajectory.

Step 5

Draw A Conclusion (Architect the Future)

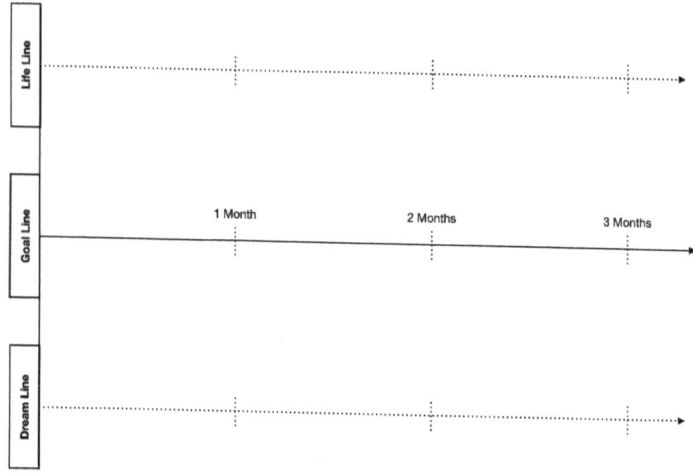

1. Design a timeline the next three months of your life or business. Make sure you pick a date by which each goal will become a reality. You need to date your goals before saying "I Do."
2. Thank yourself for doing the work. Say a prayer over your future.

CONCLUSION

After completing this process you are both psychologically and physiologically ready to take action towards the future.

As you repeat this process every three months you will get better and better at experimenting with the future. You may also notice that you discover goals and futures that are more aligned with your capabilities and capacities. You might realize that you are able to achieve things you never thought possible.

Remember there is no success or failure, only experimentation….repeat, repeat, repeat.

NOTES

NOTES

There is No Success and No Failure in an Experiment
There is Only Data and Information

CHAPTER 5 | **EXPERIMENTS**

In this chapter you will find experiments that you can run to help you discover and achieve your goals. Although these experiments are part of the Mind Lab Method, they can also be stand-alone experiments that you can perform as needed to access new states and gain new insights.

Experiment 1
Change your feelings, change your goals

Let's do an experiment to find out how your feelings change your goals.

1. Take a moment, right now, and feel the feelings of being happy, powerful and free in your body. You can start by simply thinking the words and thoughts of "happy, powerful, and free."
2. Notice how you feel different and allow your body to change as you feel the feelings of happy, powerful, and free. Notice if you want to sit, or stand, differently and how the muscles in your body change.

3. In this happy, powerful, and free state, ask yourself, "what are my goals right now?"
4. Notice what goals emerge and write them down.

Experiment 2
Get 33% Closer to your goal right now

1. Think of a goal you have over the next two weeks.
2. Now think of the feelings you will have when you accomplish the goal.
3. Find those feelings in the body right now.
4. Continue to feel those feelings of the goal and maintain that feeling, over and over again.
5. See if you can experience the entire day from the feeling of your goal being accomplished. Notice what happens.

If you did the exercise properly then you are already at least 33% of the way to achieving that goals. Yes, It can be that simple.

Experiment 3
Background Noise

Let's do an experiment to see what is running in the background of the nervous system.

1. Set a timer for 3 min.
2. Close your eyes and Take a slow inhale and then exhale.
3. Simply notice what you notice, both internally and externally. What things are stimulating your nervous system in your current internal and external environments?
4. When the timer rings, open your eyes and take a moment to write down what you noticed.

You may have become aware of pains in the body, outside stimulus or inner thoughts. All these things are stimulating the nervous system and triggering thoughts, feelings, and beliefs. Any stimulus of the nervous system is taking energy and focus in the moment.

By simply becoming aware of the nervous system and creating space between thought, feeling and action, the unconscious influence of the past becomes less significant. When we are more in touch with ourselves we make better decisions, have better ideas, and ultimately think about new future possibilities.

Experiment 4
Ask a Question About the Future

You are going to see what happens when you ask a question that you do not know the answer to. You will need a partner for this experiment, preferably someone you do not know well.

1. Pick one person to be partner A and the other to be partner B.
2. Partner A is going to ask the question, "what is the future I see for partner B." Then partner A is going to answer the question. Whatever comes to mind when you ask the question, start sharing it with partner B. This will help you activate your imagination, free from the past.
3. Partner B's job is to listen.
4. Now switch roles. Partner B will ask the same question and answer it. Partner A's job is to listen.

During this experiment people sometimes feel uncomfortable and nervous. They may not be comfortable with making things up, they may try to get the right answer, or fear getting the wrong answer. Sometimes people freeze or break into a sweat. This is all information about how our nervous system is responding to the task of make things up.

Experiment 5
Mind Dump

1. **Set a timer for 5-10 minutes**
2. Ask yourself the question, "what do I want to accomplish in the next three months." When you ask the question, answers will come to mind and then you can harvest the answers by writing them down.
3. This is a free write. The goal is not to find the right answers, rather the goal is to see what answers arise when we ask the question. When you get an answer, no matter how impossible or how simple, you write it down.
4. After the set time, review your answer to discover what is in your mind when you think about your goals and future.

Experiment 6
HeartScape

1. **Set a timer for 5-10 minutes**
2. Find your heartbeat. You may feel it on the left center of the chest, along the thumb side of the wrist or in the neck. As you become aware of your heartbeat, see if you

can feel it grow stronger in the body and notice how it can set the rhythm for the entire body.
3. As you feel your heat beat, **a**sk yourself the question, "what do I want to accomplish in the next 3-months." When you ask the question, answers will come to heart and then you can harvest the answers by writing them down.
4. This is a free write. As answers arise from the state of heart beat focus, write them down, no matter how impossible or simple they appear.
5. After the set time, review your answer to discover unique insights into what your heart wants to accomplish.

Experiment 7
Future Tripping

Part 1
1. Focus on your heart beat and close your eyes, Then ask yourself, "what is one miracle that I would like to happen in my life within the next 3-months."
2. As answers arise, select the one that you feel best about. If it happened, it would change your life forever and it would put you on a positive trajectory into the future.
3. Write that one possibility down on a piece of paper

Part 2

1. Close your eyes and take three slow, deep inhales and exhales.
2. Find your heartbeat and notice how it moves from your chest, up your neck and into your brain. Notice how your heart and brain can beat in one time and one place.
3. Allow your mind to wander into the future where your miracles has happened. Notice what you notice as you watch it happen.
4. As you realize it has already happened, notice what you are wearing, who is with you, what the environment is like, how you are standing and talking. Notice as many things as you can in that moment.
5. Now notice the feelings in the body. Notice the excitement and energy as you realize that the miracle has happened.
6. Now amplify those feelings in the body. Feel them more strongly.
7. Now imagine the first person you are going to tell about this miracle. Imagine them in front of you and say to them, "You will never believe what happened." And then see and feel yourself telling them what happened.
8. Notice how they feel for you, and how excited and happy they are for your. And notice how their feelings can amplify your feelings.
9. Again notice the feeling in your body that the thing has already happened. That future possibility has become a reality.

10. As you keep that feeling, bring you mind back into the present moment.
11. Maintain the feelings in your body in the present moment.
12. Open your eyes and harvest any new insights.

If you want to amplify this experiment even more, then find someone and tell them what happened. Remember to tell them as if it has already happened, starting with, "you will never believe what happened." Make sure you speak confidently and maintain the feeling in the body as if it has already happened.

To keep this experiment going, you simply need to keep the feeling as if it has already happened. Even though it has not happened yet, you have built a relationship with the future physiology where the possibility has become a reality. If you can maintain that physiological state your brain will continue to look for that thing to happen, and your body will maintain the posture as if it has already happened. So you increase the probability that you will see opportunities for that thing to become real and you reduce the resistance to allowing it to happen.

Experiment 8
Meet Your Future Self

Meet Your Future Self Visualization/Micro-Meditation

1. Close your eyes and take three slow, deep breaths.
2. Find your heartbeat and notice how your heartbeat moves up your neck and into your brain.
3. Bring awareness back to the heartbeat in the chest.
4. Notice a spiral of DNA expanding from your heart backwards in space and time
5. Realize that the spiral of DNA has all your life stories and experiences.
6. Allow your mind to move along that spiral of DNA backwards in space and time.
7. As you move backwards in space in time, notice any places that feel sticky or stuck. Send in love and forgiveness to those places and smooth them out.
8. Continue to move backwards in space and time along that spiral of DNA and continue to smooth it out.
9. Allow your mind to arrive at the day you are born and connect with the heartbeat of that newborn child that is you.
10. Take a deep, slow inhale. And exhale.
11. Thank yourself for being born. And realize all the potential you have and the unlimited possibilities available to you.

12. Now allow your mind to move forward in space and time along the spiral of DNA. Notice how much smoother and clearer it is now.
13. Arrive at the present moment. Take an inhale, and exhale.
14. Now allow your mind to move forward in space in time along the future timeline of your life.
15. Allow your mind to arrive at a nice, clean, crisp forest.
16. Walk around the forest and notice how it feels in your body. Notice any sounds, smells and sights. Bring your body fully into the experience.
17. As you walk through the forest you notice a house and a porch with two chairs.
18. As you get closer you realize that in one chair is an old man or an old woman. And you realize that that old man or old woman is you. The future you.
19. Sit down next to the future you and look yourself in the eyes.
20. Notice how you look in the future. How does your hair look, what clothes are you wearing, what does your face look like? Notice what you notice.
21. Now look yourself in the eyes, and ask yourself, "What do I need to know right now?"
22. Take note of whatever you hear.
23. Again ask yourself, "What do I need to know right now?"
24. And a third time, ask yourself, "What do I need to know right now?"

25. Now your future self has a gift for you. Allow your future self to hand you the gift and when you are ready, open it up to see what it is. Accept the gift without judgement.
26. Look your future self in the eyes and thank yourself.
27. Now allow your mind to move backwards in space and time to the present moment.
28. Take a slow, deep inhale. Exhale.
29. Open your eyes when you are ready.

Experiment 9
IF, THEN to I, AM

1. Write down one of your goals on a piece of paper.
2. Focus on your heart beat and ask yourself, "how could I accomplish this goal." Challenge your self to free write as many possibilities as you can, no matter how impossible or simple they seem.
3. Now select your top three pathways to achieving the goal and write them down in the form of, "If I do X (the how), Then I will achieve Y (the goal)."
4. Read the statements aloud three times each and see which one resonates, or feels the most aligned, with the future.
5. Select the best "If, Then" Statement and transform it into an "I, Am," statement.

6. For example you can transform, "If I take singing lessons, then I will be performing on stage in one month" to "I am taking singing lessons and I will perform on stage in one month."
7. Notice how you feel when you change the statement from an "If, Then" to "I, Am."

EXPERIMENT 10
Feeling the Future

Let's get to work plotting a trajectory into our future where we have become the person who has achieved the goals and feel the feelings behind the goal right now.

Here are the steps:
1. In the Box Labeled Option A write down how you will feel when you achieve your top three goals. Write those feelings in the box.
2. In the Box Labeled Option B write down how you will feel if you do not achieve your top three goals. Write those feelings in the box.
3. These are two potential future extremes that you can plot a course towards. In one future, Option A, you become the person that can achieve all your goals and dreams. In the other, option B, none of your goals and dreams become real. Notice that there are also a lot of options in between these two.

4. You want to plot the course, and stay on the course, towards Option A. To do that you need to keep our level of conscious awareness high.
5. Now draw a line from the NOW point on the bottom left of the page to Option A. This is your path to the future you want.
6. To increase awareness on how you can stay on that course, ask yourself the questions in each column and write down a few answers to each in the specified columns.
7. Remember, these questions are no longer goal focused, rather they are feeling-focused. They help us understand that there are things we can do right now to cultivate the feelings we want regardless if we achieve the goal or not.
8. Questions to ask yourself: write down three to five answers for each question
    8.1. What do I need to **release** to feel option A?
    8.2. What do I need to **learn** to feel option A?
    8.3. What do I need to **create** to feel option A?
    8.4. Who or what do I need to **connect** with to feel option A?
    8.5. What do I need to **give** to feel option A?
9. Review your answers and select one from each column that you feel matters the most.
10. Take a moment and fill out the sentence at the bottom of the page using the answers. I am releasing _____, learning _____, connecting with

_____, creating _____, and giving_____ so I can feel like _____(Option A).

11. Read the statement several times to yourself and out loud. Notice how the sentence feels when you say it. Notice if you are confident or hesitant about the words. This is a good test to see if you are ready to move into that future and the feelings it will bring.
12. If you want to amplify the experiment, read the statement out loud to someone else and have then give you feedback on how it felt to them as you read it. Were you able to share your trajectory with clarity and confidence?

NOTES

NOTES

CHAPTER 6 | 10 LESSONS LEARNED FROM HOSTING THE MIND LAB METHOD AROUND THE WORLD

In this chapter you will discover 10 of the lessons I have learned from traveling around the world and hosting **Mind Lab Method** events. Some of these lessons are based on the results of participants and some from my own personal experience. My hope is that they reinforce what you learned in the previous chapters and provide some new insights and inspirations for architecting your future and achieving your goals.

LESSON 1
When you get clear on what you want, you get what you need (Or how to lose your business and gain a life in Tokyo)

In the summer of 2016 I facilitated a **Mind Lab Method** in Tokyo, Japan. One of the attendees was a top personal development coach in Tokyo. He ran a multimillion dollar business with 20+ staff. He was very excited about the process and eager to participate and learn.

After the workshop he was impressed with the process and hinted at the idea of me training some of his coaches upon my return to Japan later that year. However, a few months after the workshop there was still no follow up from him, which is not typical of Japanese culture.

Fast forward to summer of 2017 (one year later). I was back in Tokyo to teach another round of **Mind Lab Method** workshops. To my surprise, the coach who attended the 2016 event showed up for another session. I inquired, "why have you returned when you already took the class last year?"

He was excited to announce that all his 2016 **Mind Lab Method** goals materialized exactly as he had written them down and on the exact dates he specified. He was shocked, and he wanted to see if he could repeat the success.

To my further surprise, he continued to explain that his company almost went bankrupt and he had to layoff more than half of his staff. He was now in the process of rebuilding his business. I was shocked by the story, yet he seemed excited, energized, and was showing up for another go at the **Mind Lab Method**.

I asked him what goals he set to bring about such a drastic change. He explained that during the **Mind Lab Method** he realized that his life and his business were moving in different directions. Although his business was very successful, it was not aligned with his personal life and his personal vision of the future. After gaining clarity, he used the tools provided during the **Mind Lab Method** to make tangible changes fast.

He got clear on what he wanted, and so he got what he needed to make the desired future real. And part of what he needed was to scale back his company and recalibrate. This might seem like a setback at first, but it allowed him to get on the right trajectory into the right future.

Sometimes the things we need in life are not always obvious to us. When we gain clarity on what we want, we might discover that the path there seems unpleasant. Getting clear about the future opens us up to uncertainty, change, and the risk of failure in life or business. All this can seem scary to our brain and overall physiology.

However, in the long run, getting clear on what you want will help you get what you really need. In the short term this might cause things to stop working like they did in the past. What got you to where you are today, might not be the best strategy to move you into the future. As you let go of the past, new trajectories can emerge which will benefit your life and business in the long-term.

The Tokyo coach has happily grown a new, successful company aligned with his life and vision, and although the change almost cost him his whole company, it was worth it because in the long run he got his life back.

Lesson learned: It is important to get clear about what you want in the future, and then allow the things you need to materialize, even if it is not what you are expecting.

LESSON 2
The path to your goals is right in front of you. (Or how to achieve your goal in two hours or less)

As we discussed earlier in the book, scientific studies have show that clarity is one of the superpowers to achieving your goals. For example, "I want to make more money" is not a good goal. There is no clarity about when, how, or why. The brain wants to support us in achieving our goals, but it needs direction.

So you tell your brain to "make more money" and it finds a penny on the street and it thinks it has done the job you asked. I like to think of the brain as a loyal dog. If you teach him to fetch he will do it for hours. Show your dog how to sit and he loves that he can sit for you. However, if you are like me, you know that training a dog is not easy. It takes consistent clarity over time, and training repetition to get the dog to understand your desired outcome. In the same way, the brain requires consistent clarity of thought and action to direct it to accomplish the what, where, when, how, and why of what you want.

I recall a girl in one of the Los Angeles **Mind Lab Method** events using the power of clarity and the future tripping experiment (*Experiment 7*) to make a "miracle" happen in two hours.

During the future tripping experiment she envisioned a future where she was learning videography and was working with the perfect mentor. In the experiment she saw and felt a future with (1) someone who was focused on documentary film, (2) someone that was looking for a person to mentor and needed immediate help and, (3) someone who lives within a few miles of here home (very important in Los Angeles to avoid traffic). As she ran this clear vision through the future tripping experiment she built a physiological relationship with the future where the miracle had already happened.

Interestingly, at that particular **Mind Lab Method** event we had a videographer filming for us. At the end of the event the girl casually started talking to him and quickly realized that he was focused on documentary film, he was looking for someone to mentor and needed help now, and the most surprising, he lived only a few blocks from her home in Los Angeles. All three of her criteria met within less than two hours of getting clear on what she wanted.

Seems like a "miracle" to me.

When we get clear on what we want, then our brain, just like a loyal dog, will do its best make it a reality. And when we get clear, we might realize that what we want is right in front of us, but we could not see it because our brain did not know we were looking for it. Using the power of clarity, along with the future tripping experiment, the brain and body are preloaded with the desired outcome and know exactly what to look for to make the goal a reality.

Lesson Learned: Train the brain to look for exactly what you want through the power of clarity and future tripping, and then allow the brain to find it. When you train the brain to see properly, you might realize what you want is right in front of you.

LESSON 3
Thinking about the future is not easy (Or how increasing your brainpower is like yoga practice)

Most people are not thinking enough about their goals. They might be taking action, but still not achieving what they want and wasting valuable time and energy. I recall a **Mind Lab Method** in Sacramento, California where one attendee became very frustrated with the process because she did not have mental stamina.

When tasked with using the Power of Writing during the workshop, her brain could not generate anything, just a blank stare. She knew the process was important for her and wanted to complete it, but she just did not have the brainpower required.

Walter Russell who was the advisor for IBM in the 1950s says, "I have always made it a rule to get my prospect's signature in my head before I get it on paper, for I feel certain that when I have so perfectly designed the pattern of my sale that my imagination sees it all signed up, it gives me a mental attitude that assures the signature later. I cannot stress the importance of this too much to you young salesmen who are getting your training here." [14]

If we do not have the brain power to think about the future, then we are not fully conscious of the future you are creating. Thinking about your future and your goals is just like a physical work out or a yoga practice. When you first start yoga you might be weak, lack flexibility, and unaware of certain mind-body connections. As you continue to develop your practice over months, you grow the muscles, stamina, flexibility, and mental power to practice more efficiently and effectively.

---

[14] Russell, Walter. THINK - WALTER RUSSELL IBM LECTURE SERIES (Kindle Location 2454). University of Science and Philosophy. Kindle Edition.

Interestingly, it is a challenge for the brain to think about the future. It is highly concerned with what happens in the next five seconds, constantly predicting if an immediate threat to survival might arise. But, for the brain, thinking about what happens tomorrow or in the next three months or five years is a waste of energy. To make matters worse, as we think further into the future it becomes more and more scary to the brain because ultimately the future leads to death.

For the brain, survival in the moment is the ultimate goal and death is one of its biggest enemies. You must train your brain to go beyond these limitations.

The techniques shared in this book are designed to help you improve your future-thinking brain power. As you gain the stamina to think about the future and hold that vision of the future in your mind and body more consistently, then you become better at architecting your future. If your brain power is too weak to do the work, then you need to practice thinking about the future and stretching the mind to increase your capacity and capabilities.

Just as Walter Russell says, you have to practice thinking about the future as much as you practice taking action toward the future. When you thinking and acting are in balance then you are more coherent in your efforts in creating the future and you are more efficient and effective with your time and energy.

Several months after the Sacramento event I was in Oakland hosting another **Mind Lab Method** event. Surprisingly, the girl from Sacramento who had difficulty finding the brainpower to finish the process had returned for a second class. She had stretched her brain and increased its power and was ready to give her future a second chance. This time she completed the process and felt very good with the results. She was overcoming the limitations of the brain and expanding her ability to consciously architect the future.

Remember, if you are not creating your future, then someone with more brainpower is creating it for you.

Lesson Learned: You have to practice thinking about the future as much as you practice taking action toward the future. Often this requires you to exercise your brain (like yoga for the mind) to increase your capabilities and capacity to think about the future.

LESSON 4
You are the biggest barrier to achieving your goals (Or how to become the future you)

In 2009 I co-founded a media company called Nella Media Group. It was typical for budding entrepreneurs to visit our office and tell us about their big ideas. I recall one day sitting in the office talking with an aspiring entrepreneur and the theme of the conversation was "if I just had more time, more money, a team, and your support, we could make millions." Since then I have heard variations on this theme over and over again.

Interestingly, we were sitting in an office of a media company that was started with no time, no money, and no team. The first month of business operations we were asking ourselves, "how are we going to afford this office?" We currently did not have the funds to afford the next month's payment and the minimal work we did have was not going to cover the rent.

My business partner and I realized we had two skill sets to leverage, (1) we both had strong networks of friends and business acquaintances and (2) we both knew how to throw events. So we created a monthly event in Honolulu called EcoLounge with the goal of bringing together the action sports and sustainable lifestyle networks. The event was a hit and it paid our rent, not only for that first month, but for the next two years.

My business partner and I had a company motto, "we get things done." That was the type of people we wanted to be. The entrepreneur in the office talking about how he needs more time, money, a team (and my support) to achieve his goals is not the person who can get things done. He has to change himself internally first and realize that external limitations do not matter.

Lack of time, money, or a team are never a barrier to your goals. The barrier is you. The person you are right now, the physiology you have practiced to create your state of being, and the preprogrammed habits and behaviors you have anchored in your subconscious are the limiting factors.

One thing people fail to realize is that you have to become a different person to achieve your goals. That is why they are called goals. No matter how much time, money, or how big your team is, if you are not willing to change then you cannot achieve the goal.

During the first year of operations my media company was designing ads for a local airlines. The marketing director for the airlines commented on how they were looking for a new publisher of their inflight magazine, the second most read publication in Hawai'i. We quickly responded with, "we can publish it."

They asked us to submit a proposal and a week later we received the confirmation that we had won the contract over several other well-established companies.

We were excited to have our first big opportunity as a media company and while we were celebrating the contract I remember my business partner turning to me and saying, "you are going to be the editor." (He was a marketing and sales guy).

My first thought was, "what does an editor do?" I picked up an old inflight magazine and looked at the masthead, where they listed the names of at least 20 people who had contributed to the publication, including the editor. My second thought was, "how are we going to do this?" Our company consisted of my business partner and I, and a part-time designer. We had no team.

I immediately called up two friends to ask for advice and help. One was a freelance writer and the other was an assistant editor for a magazine. During the conversation I informed them that I was now the editor for the second most read publication in Hawai'i and I was wondering if they could help me understand what an editor does. They both laughed as if I was telling them a joke, but it was no joke. To make things more interesting, the next issue of the in-flight magazine was due in the airplane seats in just over one month.

I did not have the luxury to say, "I need more time, more money and more resources." I did not have time to think about the fact that the role I now had to play would typically take years of study and real life experience to master. Four years of college studying writing or journalism, followed by writing jobs and assistant editor positions, until one day, maybe after a minimum of 8-10 years, you become the editor of the second most read publication in Hawai'i.

I had to become an editor overnight. I immediately started doing what editors do and within one-month the first issue of the in-flight magazine was in the seats of the plane. I was an editor.

So ask yourself, "who is the person I need to become to achieve the goal?" and, "what would I be doing right now if I had already achieved the goal?"

Start taking the steps right now to change yourself into that person. Remove your focus away from the goal and focus on becoming the new you with new feelings, new clothes, and new ways of being. Become the person that makes things happen by changing their inner world regardless of what the external world looks like.

Lesson Learned: Lack of time, money, or resources are not the barrier to your future. You are the barrier to your future. Start doing the new you right now.

LESSON 5
You have to have one clear vision of the future (Or how to miss a flight to a conference)

If you really want to be a Jedi of creating your future, you need to have one clear future to aim at. When you have goals and futures that conflict they can cause real problems in your life.

For example, a friend had been timelining his future using the **Mind Lab Method** and landed an opportunity to speak at a conference in Europe. Interestingly, his goal-setting work had also landed him an opportunity to speak at a second conference in California. The one problem was the conferences were on the same weekend, so he could not attend both.

In this mind he strongly desired to attend both conferences as they seemed equally valuable and exciting. He needed to make a choice, timeline out the one clear future he wanted, and let go of the other future possibility.

However, he could not choose. Although he started to make plans for the European conference and had the organizers book his flight and hotel, he still wanted to keep open the possibility to attend the other conference in Los Angeles. His mind was in two futures.

The morning of his flight to Europe he was still conflicted in his physiology and wanted to be in both futures. At this point he had continually been sending mixed messages to his physiology about which future to prepare for and which future he wanted his body to be in.

When we do this an interesting thing happens. Our brain wants to help us and give us exactly what we want. So when we want to leave open a possibility our brain does everything it can to help us keep that possibility open. So what kinds of things can a brain do to help us out?

Consider this, if you tell yourself you are always late for meetings, then you are sending a message to the brain that you want to be late for meetings. So your brain, being the good friend it is, helps you out. When you are getting ready for a meeting it will make it difficult for you to be ready on time.

Maybe your brain-body will hide your car keys in a drawer, or maybe your car keys are right in front of you but you brain will not let you see them, because you are always late for meetings. Or maybe you are going to be on time for the meeting and your body helps you to be late by knocking over a glass of water and causing a mess that you have to clean up so you can be late. Or maybe it helps you take a wrong turn on the ride over to the meeting so you can show up late. Because you are the type of person that is always late for meetings, your brain will help you be truthful and support what you want.

So my friend wants to be at both the conference in Europe and the one in Los Angeles, but they are on the same weekend and he cannot be at both. It is the day of the plane flight to Europe and still he wants to leave open the possibility to attend the conference in Los Angeles sending, a mixed signal to the body and brain about what future he wants to be in.

What does his brain do?

It gladly helps him keep open the possibility to attend either conference by reading the flight time incorrectly so he can show up two hours late for the flight. He is not new to traveling, as he travels often for work, so missing the flight is not the norm. I was meeting with him the morning of the flight and I recall asking him his flight time and seeing him look at the flight details that morning and still his brain got it wrong, by two hours.

The other way to think about it is that his brain got the time correct. It helped him leave open the possibility of attending either event. The future was still unclear and undetermined in his mind and so he missed his flight so his future could remain uncertain.

Not choosing one clear future cost him. He ended up deciding to attend the conference in Europe, because it was really the better option in the end. But he had to pay his own plane ticket and one of his presentations was cut from the programing. Maybe he missed out on a bigger opportunity.

Lesson Learned: Be clear about the one future you want. This will help your brain and body align to that future. If you send the brain and body mixed signals it will help you to stay in an uncertain and indecisive state.

LESSON 6
Miracles do happen (Or how to find a date and get married in three months)

After completing a three month West Coast tour with the **Mind Lab Method** I wanted to expand my own future intelligence. I started to experiment with the idea of how to make miracles in the future more likely to happen. One strategy, that also become a key component of the **Mind Lab Method**, is thinking, feeling, and acting as if a miracle has already happened to increase the probability that it will happen.

I ran a personal experiment using this process to see if it

would be possible to land a speaking engagement at a company in Kuala Lumpur called Mind Valley. If you do not know Mind Valley they are one of the largest online distributors of personal development training material.

Prior to the experiment, I had no contacts at Mind Valley, I had only been a fan of their work. I used the Mind Lab technique to create a three month timeline at the end of which I would be speaking at Mind Valley, and then amplified that future possibility by thinking, feeling and acting if that future had already become a reality.

Within a couple weeks I met two people who had direct connection to the Mind Valley CEO. Within two months I was talking on Skype with the Mind Valley in-house education team and in three months, just as I had written on my timeline, I was in the offices of Mind Valley. The miracle had happened in three months just as I had planned.

Well, not exactly.

To be honest I did not get to speak to their employees during my first visit, that actually happened a month later when I returned to Kuala Lumpur to visit Mind Valley for the second time. Still, I went from a goal that I thought initially had only a slim chance of happening, to completing that goal in four months.

I have seen these types of "miracles" happen again and again after people attend the **Mind Lab Method**. One attendee from Japan was intent on getting married, however she was having a difficult time finding someone to even date. She wanted to see if she could use the Mind Lab Method not only to get married, but to get married in three months. I don't know about you, but the idea of finding someone to date, that you like enough to marry, in three months, seems impossible. I guess that is my limiting belief.

She went through the **Mind Lab Method** and architected a future where she was married three months later. I reminder her that she needed to live as if that future was a reality and I challenged her to start doing the things she would do if she was already married. That meant embodying the person she would be in the future where she was married.

One month later I was notified that she was dating someone who was also at the same Mind Lab event. They were planning to get married just as she had specified on here three month timeline. Three months later, I was notified that they were married. Miracles do happen.

Lesson learned: When you align your entire physiology to a specific future, even if that future is a miracle, you increase the probability that it will become a reality.

LESSON 7
Sometimes the small, intangible goals matter most (Or how to fall In love again)

When we think about goals we tend to think about tangible and external achievements in life or business. However, sometimes it is the small goals that matter the most because they can help us realign our internal compass and discover a bigger and brighter future.

I was hosting the **Mind Lab Method** at an entrepreneur and creativity event in California called Camp Unique. One of the attendees I met had already accomplished many things in life as a production manager for a very successful musician. Now he was looking for his next big thing.

I recall him coming up to me four hours after the **Mind Lab Method** event and with much excitement, telling me about a huge insight he had.

What struck him as the most important goal in his life right now was to learn how to fall in love again. It had been at least five years since he had felt love in the way he wanted to feel it from another person. He proceeded to tell me that after the event he sat down on a bench to write and reflect on the experience. As he was sitting there a girl approached him and said, "do you mind if I join you on the bench." He said, "OK," and she sat down and they started talking. He recalled that after the conversation with the girl, he had found the internal feeling of being able to fall in love again.

This girl was not his one true love (although that would have been really interesting). But the **Mind Lab Method** allowed him to gain insight into one simple thing that was missing in his life, and the conversation he had after the workshop allowed him to find the feeling that he could let go of the past and fall in love again in the future. From that simple exchange he felt as if his entire life had moved in a new and positive direction. He was ready for the next big thing.

Lesson Learned: When it comes to goals, do not neglect the small, intangible ones.

LESSON 8
You can accomplish 10 year goals in four months (Or how to launch a festival, fast)

During a **Mind Lab** in Los Angeles we had a recent college graduate who was both very enthusiastic and confused about her next steps in life. She was wondering if she should get a job or follow some other passion. She briefly mentioned a goal that had been on her mind for many months, but for some reason she thought it was 10 years away from becoming a reality.

The idea was to create an arts and music festival that would happen in the desert of California around the concept of Unconditional Love. I challenged her by asking, "what if that 10 year goal could be achieved in three months? What would that look like?"

She had never thought about it that way before and was skeptical of the time frame. In her mind there were many things that had to happen in her life for her to complete the goal. She thought she needed more life experience, needed to build a network in her niche, and then save money to fund the event.

One interesting thing is that the perceived path to our goals can be a limitation on a achieving the goal. If you think it will take 10 years to complete a goal, then that is a barrier to completing it faster. It is typical that we think we need more time, more money, more learning or more resources to achieve our goals in life, but that is not always true.

The strategies we choose to achieve our goal can also limit us. For example, to become a yoga instructor most people think they need to complete 200-hr Registered Yoga

Teacher training (RYT), certified by Yoga Alliance to teach yoga. If that is your strategy to become a yoga teacher, then you have to follow that strategy to get there. There is no reason why you cannot think of other strategies. For example, many great yoga teachers, especially the ones I have personally met from India, are not 200Hr RYT certified.

I experimented with different strategies to find my path to becoming a yoga teacher. I opted for a 40 hour training in Ashtanga from a well respected teacher, David Swenson. After that training, I considered myself a teacher and started teaching yoga in Hawai'i and China.

Once you discover a goal you need to ask yourself, "does my perceived strategy to achieve that goal limit me?" It is important to take time and discover the strategies that can help you reach your goal, and also help you reach your goal in a way that aligns with your capabilities and mindstate. If you think achieving the goal should be difficult and take 10 years to complete, then you will develop a strategy that allows the process to be difficult and take 10 years to complete.

One of the best ways to discover new strategies to achieving your goals is to ask other people, especially people who do not know you, how you could achieve the goal. They will not be able to think themselves into the same boxes and limitations that you have for yourself.

Their ideas will challenge you and inspire you. And of course some of their ideas will not be useful at all.

I challenged the Los Angeles participant to ask herself, "what if I could achieve my 10 year goal in three months?" She applied that thinking to the Mind Lab process and then waited to see what would happen. Three months latter I ran into her at an event in Los Angeles and she was ecstatic to report that the event was going to happen in just one more month.

She was able to overcome the limitations of her thinking and turn a 10 year goal into a four month reality.

What strategies do you have that are limiting you from achieving your goals and how can you shift your thinking right now to discover new strategies to achieve your goals faster?

Lesson Learned: You can make things happen faster than you think you can. Don't let your strategies to the future limit what is possible.

LESSON 9
The future Is bigger than you can imagine (Or how to become an Eagle)

One of my favorite stories is the Native American tale (tribe unknown) of Jumping Mouse. One day a mouse hears a sound and decides to follow it. It leads him to a river where he is shown the sacred mountains and receives a new name, Jumping Mouse.

Jumping mouse decides to leave his home and journey to the sacred mountains. Along the journey to the sacred mountains the mouse gives away both his eyes. One eye heals a bison and the other heals a wolf. In exchange jumping mouse is protected from the shadow of the eagles and guided to the top of the sacred mountains.

At the top of the mountain the blind mouse sits in fear, waiting for an eagle to snatch him up. But instead he hears a voice that says, "crouch as low as you can and jump as high as you can, and you will have your medicine power."

Little jumping mouse has nothing to loose, and so he crouches as low as he can and jumps as high as he can. As he soars higher and higher he feels himself become one with the wind.

He hears the voice again say, "Jumping mouse, you have a new name, it is Eagle."

This story illustrates the fact that the future you are preparing for is probably bigger than you can imagine right now. The little mouse simply wanted to see the sacred mountains, that was his goal. He did not realize that in the process he would become blind to the past and ultimately transform into something he could never imagine. He actually became the very thing that he feared the most, the eagle. Once he becomes the eagle, a whole new world opens up, with new possibilities and futures.

Keep this in mind as you think about your future and your goals. What you are imagining right now is only the beginning of something much bigger. The person you are right now cannot even imagine what is really waiting for you because your imagination is limited either by the past or by the current perspective from which you currently view the world. As you take action toward your goal and become a new person, new ideas and possibilities, that you never imagined before, will arise.

You don't need faith or belief that there is something bigger and better. As you grow and develop new visions of the future and take action towards them, *you will* also grown and developed into something new. This is just a fact.

In my experience, when I take a leap towards a goal, I know that it is leading me to something I cannot even imagine right now. Even though I know the goal will become obsolete, I still stay focused on the goal, just as Jumping Mouse stayed focused on getting to the top of the sacred mountain.

Small steps with consistent focus allows you to go blind to the past so you can embody a new future. As the new future emerges, you can imagine new things that were not available to you when you started the journey. Jumping Mouse could never imagine becoming an Eagle.

Ask yourself, "what could I never imagine becoming?" Maybe that will be the start of your next journey.

Lesson Learned: What you imagine in the future right now is only the beginning. There is much more waiting for you.

LESSON 10
Achieving your goals is like going home

What if achieving your goals was just like going home?

Imagine you are leaving work or the gym on your way home. Maybe you stop somewhere along the way, maybe you take a wrong turn, or maybe you get stuck in traffic and it takes longer to get home than expected. But still, you get home.

You don't stop half way and give up. You don't accidentally arrive at the wrong home. You don't forget the way home and end up working on a different goal. And even if you are thousands of miles away, if you need to get home you will do everything you can, no matter the cost or effort, to get there.

What if you treated your goals like going home? You don't stop halfway, you don't let a wrong turn or a delay stop you. You don't give up on the goal and focus on something else and you don't accidentally complete the wrong goal.

When you change your mindset and treat your goals like going home then you will know the path to achieve them and you will not give up along the way. Yes, it can be that easy.

Lesson Learned: Treat your goals just like going home.

NOTES

NOTES

*If You Are Not Creating Your Future
Then Someone Is Creating It For You*

CONCLUSION | THE FUTURE IS AN EXPERIMENT

One approach that I stress in the **Mind Lab Method** is to treat your goals and future like an experiment. This allows you to access the power of the Scientific Method and also removes the concerns of failure or the attachment to success.

During college I worked at the Medical College of Georgia researching the effects of site-directed mutagenesis on the DNA of sugar transporter proteins of parasitic protozoa. This simply means I mutated the DNA of the protein to see how the mutation would effect the absorption of sugar into the parasite cells. Sometimes the experiments supported our hypothesis and sometimes they did not.

One thing you learn in research is you cannot be attached to the results. You create a hypothesis, a theory about what might happen, and then you test it and see what results you get. You collect the data, regardless if it supported your hypothesis or not, and you report the results. Both

Positive and negative results help to build a body of knowledge that can be a foundation for future studies.

The best science results from unbiased and objective perspective of the results without a concern for success or failure. You test the idea, collect date and repeat until the experiment can provide a consistent and repeatable outcome.

This type of thinking can have a profound effect on our goals.

Often times during the goal-setting process our brain will think of a goal, and then quickly see failure. Thoughts like, "I can't do that," "it is going to be too difficult," "it will take too much time," and so on, prevent us from committing to a goal or future. When we see failure, the brain is uncomfortable and so we often choose goals and futures that seem comfortable, have low risk and require little change in our life or physiology.

The focus on success can also limit your ability to discover and achieve the best goals. As you take action towards your goals, the future changes and emerges. Maybe new goals and ideas of your future self emerge in the process. Maybe achieving your initial goal does not matter. Rather you learn how to enjoy the process and how to discover the feelings behind the goal.

When you start to think about your goals as an experiment, then you can set your goals and start moving toward them without the fear of failure or the pressures of success. If you achieve that 10 year goal in three months, then great. Collect the data, recalibrate and repeat the process. If you do not achieve your 10 year goal in 3 months, then great. Collect the data, recalibrate and repeat the process.

As you embrace the scientific approach to goal setting and future creation, then your life and business can have a nice balance between structure and flow. You are inquisitive and curious about what is possible in your life and you can design and strategize your future without pressure. Once you have set the experiment, you let it run and flow with life and then see what results you get when the experiment is completed. You collect the new information and gain new awareness of your self and the world, and then you repeat the process.

One of the key lessons learned from hosting **Mind Lab Method** events around the world is that Your goals don't matter. What matters is the feelings behind the goals. The best thing about feelings is you can activate them in your body right now.

Let's try this experiment, which you may recall from the beginning of this book. Think the thought, "happy." As you think "happy", notice what happens in your body.

Notice how the simple thought of "happy" activates feelings in the body that encourage you to take actions that are associated with being happy.

Thoughts stimulate feelings in the body. These feelings are directly related to the neural-chemical responses in the body due to the thought. As we experience life we begin to link thoughts and feelings to specific actions, further stimulating neural pathways in the body. When you think "happy", you might smile really big or even become more engaging with the people around you. You become a different person, a happy person.

As we practice the thought-feeling-action-belief loop over and over again we create a state of being in our nervous system. You may have a friend who is always happy and everyone enjoys being around. This is an expression of their state of being that is a culmination of the thoughts-feelings-actions-beliefs they have practiced throughout their life.

It is the state of being that determines what ideas we can have, what decisions we can make, and what futures we want to create.

The world of a happy person is different than the world of a stressed person. And that happy person or stressed person can be different state of your own being. This means that the happy you has a very different future than the stressed you.

If you continue with the same thought-feeling-action-belief loop then you get the same results and you are on the trajectory to a predetermined future and your goals don't matter. You have to change and activate new thoughts, new feelings and new beliefs to take new action to create a different future and achieve your goals.

Feelings are a good place to start, because you can activate feelings right now to engage the body in a new experience.

Consider this again, if you always felt happy, powerful and free, what types of goals would you have? Feel happy, powerful, and free in your body right now and then ask yourself, "what are my goals in this state?"

If you are like me, then when you feel happy, powerful and free, you don't really need much. And when you don't need much, then goals become less important or the types of goals you have are very different than the the goals you thought in the past.

When you feel happy, powerful, and free, do you think it would be easier to accomplish your goals? And don't you think that any goal that aligns with those feelings is going to be easy to accomplish?

Goals are a journey, not a destination. When you find the feeling behind your goals and then activate that feeling in the body, then in some way you have already achieved the goal. When you maintain the feeling in the body as if the goal has already happened, then the goal becomes easier to achieve with less effort and in a shorter timeframe.

Goals are important and they have value, but not in the way we typically think about them. Rather they are enlightening us to feelings we want to embody, new possibilities in the future that we want to realize, and ultimately to a new person we want to become. As we strive toward a goal and become a new person, our goals may change and that is OK, because they are not what we really wanted in the first place.

Goals are not the end, rather they are a journey into the unknown and emerging future self.

I invite you to start "Feeling the Future" and hope that your future be preferred and purposeful. Be Happy. Feel Powerful. Live Free.

Aloha.

NOTES

NOTES

NOTES

NOTES

Citations

1. Allen, James (1902). *As a Man Thinketh*.
2. Childre, Doc & Howard Martin, Deborah Rozman, Rollin McCraty (2016). *Heart Intelligence: Connecting with the Intuitive Guidance of the Heart*. U.S.A.: Waterfront Press
3. DeMartini, John (2013). *The Values Factor: The Secret to Creating an Inspired and Fulfilling Life*. U.S.A.: Berkley
4. Dispenza, Joe (2014). *You Are The Placebo: Making Your Mind Matter*. U.S.A: Hay House Inc.
5. Elgin, Duane (2009). *The Living Universe: Where Are We? Who Are We? Where Are We Going?* U.S.A: Berrett-Koehler Publishers
6. Keller, Gary & Jay Papasan *(2013) The One Thing*. U.S.A. Bard Press
7. Lipton, Bruce (2005). *The Biology Of Belief: Unleashing The Power Of Consciousness, Matter And Miracles*. U.S.A: Authors Pub Corp
8. Maltz, Maxwell (2015) *Psycho-Cybernetics: Updated and Expanded*. U.S.A.: TarcherPerigee;
9. Mcttagart, Lynn (2008). *The Intention Experiment: Using Your Thoughts to Change Your Life and the World*. U.S.A: Atria Books
10. Pearsall, Paul (1999). *The Heart's Code: Tapping the Wisdom and Power of Our Heart Energy*. U.S.A. Broadway Books
11. Sheldrake, Rupert *(2005). A New Science of Life*. U.K.: Icon Books Ltd.
12. Siegel, Daniel (2016). *Mind: A Journey Into the Heart of Being Human*. U.S.A.: W. W. Norton & Company
13. Targ, Russell (2004). *Limitless Mind: A Guide to Remote Viewing and Transformation of Consciousness*. U.S.A.: New World Library

Acknowledgements

A special thanks to Jonathan Fritzler who co-created the Mind Lab Experiment with me. And one million thanks to all the past, present and future participants in the Mind Lab Method. May all your futures be purposeful.

ABOUT THE AUTHOR

Tyler P. Mongan is an entrepreneur, biomedical researcher, and corporate leadership trainer. He spent over 3 years traveling the world sharing the Mind Lab Method: the Science of Goal Setting. Currently he trains leaders and organizations on the application of brain-heart coherence science, mindful innovation, and future intelligence. Tyler enjoys teaching yoga, practicing bagua, picking the banjo, and surfing in Hawaii. You can find out more at: www.haku.global, www.tylermongan.com & www.mindlabmethod.com

www.ingramcontent.com/pod-product-compliance
Lightning Source LLC
Chambersburg PA
CBHW070145100426
42743CB00013B/2821